# ROUTLEDGE LIBRARY EDITIONS: CHINESE LITERATURE AND ARTS

Volume 9

# A COLLECTION OF CHINESE LYRICS

# A COLLECTION OF CHINESE LYRICS

Rendered into Verse by
Alan Ayling

from translations of the Chinese by
Duncan Mackintosh

ALAN AYLING
and
DUNCAN MACKINTOSH

Taylor & Francis Group

LONDON AND NEW YORK

First published in 1965 by Routledge and Kegan Paul Ltd

This edition first published in 2022
by Routledge
4 Park Square, Milton Park, Abingdon, Oxon OX14 4RN

and by Routledge
605 Third Avenue, New York, NY 10158

*Routledge is an imprint of the Taylor & Francis Group, an informa business*

© 1965 Alan Ayling and Duncan Mackintosh

All rights reserved. No part of this book may be reprinted or reproduced or utilised in any form or by any electronic, mechanical, or other means, now known or hereafter invented, including photocopying and recording, or in any information storage or retrieval system, without permission in writing from the publishers.

Trademark notice: Product or corporate names may be trademarks or registered trademarks, and are used only for identification and explanation without intent to infringe.

*British Library Cataloguing in Publication Data*
A catalogue record for this book is available from the British Library

ISBN: 978-0-367-11183-0 (Set)
ISBN: 978-1-032-19549-0 (Volume 9) (hbk)
ISBN: 978-1-032-19550-6 (Volume 9) (pbk)
ISBN: 978-1-003-25972-5 (Volume 9) (ebk)

DOI: 10.4324/9781003259725

**Publisher's Note**
The publisher has gone to great lengths to ensure the quality of this reprint but points out that some imperfections in the original copies may be apparent.

**Disclaimer**
The publisher has made every effort to trace copyright holders and would welcome correspondence from those they have been unable to trace.

*A Collection of*
# CHINESE LYRICS

*Rendered into Verse by*
ALAN AYLING

*from translations of the Chinese by*
DUNCAN MACKINTOSH

Foreword by F. T. CHENG

Calligraphy by LEE YIM *and
on the illustrations by*
CHANG CHIEN YING

*Illustrations by*
FEI CH'ENG WU

**LONDON**
Routledge and Kegan Paul

*First published 1965
by Routledge and Kegan Paul Ltd
Broadway House, 68–74 Carter Lane
London, E.C.4*

*Printed in Great Britain
by Butler and Tanner Ltd
Frome and London*

© *Alan Ayling and Duncan Mackintosh 1965*

*No part of this book may be reproduced
in any form without permission from
the publisher, except for the quotation
of brief passages in criticism*

*To*
*Our Chinese Friends*

# FOREWORD

*by* F. T. CHENG

*Member of the Permanent Court of Arbitration,
former Ambassador to the Court of St. James, etc.*

THE TRANSLATOR OF THE POEMS in this volume has lived in China and studied in Chinese colleges. As a result he took a deep interest in Chinese literature and in Chinese poetry in particular, which across the centuries the Chinese, owing partly to their way of life and partly to their temperament, have produced in abundance, and which is still an everyday means of exchanging sentiments between scholars. As the authors themselves have in their commentary pointed out there are in Chinese literature different forms of poetry in vogue, one of which is called *Tz'u*, and this specially appeals to them; because its style is unique to the realm of Chinese poetry, and, perhaps, because it has, probably, never been introduced in any quantity into the English language, though poetry of the classical form has been translated into English by many noted scholars.

A remarkable feature of the translation of the poems embodied in this volume is that, as far as possible, the authors, while conforming to the rules of English poetry, follow the poetical texture of the original, so that the reader may have an adequate idea of what Chinese poetry is like. This is salutary. For if the translation appears in the form of prose, however beautiful it may be, it reads, after all, like prose, missing the ornament peculiar to poetry, being then like presenting a king without his crown or a priest without his gown.

In a larger sense this is also a means of widening the cultural understanding between nations; for if Chinese poetry can be rendered into the form of English poetry, 'without (of course) sacrificing perspicuity to ornament', as Pope warns in his Design to his *Essay on Man*, a Western reader will find that even in the field of literature there is much affinity between the East and the West.

The authors in their Preface have modestly said, 'If any such readers succeed in sharing the moods and feelings in these poems to the extent that they are encouraged to look further, this book's purpose will have been served.' Having read these poems, I may well say that they can be sure that this modest wish of theirs will be fulfilled.

# CONTENTS

| | |
|---|---|
| Foreword by F. T. Cheng | *page* vii |
| Preface | xi |
| Acknowledgements | xv |

### T'ANG DYNASTY

| | |
|---|---|
| Li Po | 3 |
| Po Chü I | 11 |
| Wen T'ing Yün | 17 |

### FIVE DYNASTIES

| | |
|---|---|
| Nan T'ang Chung Chu (Li Ying) | 23 |
| Nan T'ang Hou Chu (Li Yü) | 29 |

### SUNG DYNASTY

| | |
|---|---|
| Fan Chung Yen | 71 |
| Yeh Ch'ing Ch'en | 79 |
| Yen Shu | 83 |
| Yen Chi Tao | 89 |
| Ou Yang Hsiu | 93 |
| Liu Yung | 107 |
| Su Shih | 111 |
| Huang T'ing Chien | 125 |
| Ch'in Kuan | 131 |
| Chou Pang Yen | 137 |
| Li Ch'ing Chao | 143 |

### SOUTHERN SUNG DYNASTY

| | |
|---|---|
| Yüeh Fei | *page* 151 |
| Lu Yu | 155 |
| Hsin Ch'i Chi | 159 |
| Chiang K'uei | 169 |
| Liu K'o Chuang | 177 |
| Wu Wen Ying | 181 |
| Chiang Chieh | 185 |

### YÜAN DYNASTY

| | |
|---|---|
| Sa Tu La | 191 |

### MING DYNASTY

| | |
|---|---|
| Liu Chi (Po Wen) | 199 |

### CH'ING DYNASTY

| | |
|---|---|
| Na-lan Hsing-te | 205 |
| Tso Fu | 211 |
| Note on the Tz'u—its Development and Ornamentation | 214 |
| Appendix I—A Brief Historical Background to the Tz'u | 227 |
| Appendix II—Notes on Poems | 232 |
| Appendix III—Tune-patterns | 245 |
| Appendix IV—Pronunciation of Chinese Names occurring in the English poems | 249 |
| Index | 251 |

# PREFACE

UNIQUE AMONG LANGUAGES used by the great civilizations of early history, Chinese has survived and matured through at least three thousand years, to be used today by a population which, we are told, will provide one out of every four people on earth by the end of this century.

Yet little of the vast treasure of Chinese literature has been translated for the English speaking public. Of course, it is one thing to translate, another to do so acceptably. Some of us recall early translations from the Russians which suggested more the behaviour of another species than common human experience superbly observed. We have been luckier in quality, if not in quantity, with our translators from the Chinese, even though some from the past century may read a little quaintly today. But it must be admitted that the Chinese language, and through this their literature, has been neglected. There still remains for the English mind the picture of a remote, inscrutable and probably incomprehensible people with too difficult a language and too alien a tradition.

It is a pity, and may one day prove to have been in the nature of a tragedy, that more young people have not followed the example set by George Thomas Staunton who, at the age of twelve, accompanied Lord Macartney on his embassy to China in 1793 and of whom the ambassador wrote:

> Little Staunton was able to supply my wants on this occasion; for having very early in the voyage begun to study the Chinese (language) under my two interpreters, he had not only made considerable progress in it, but he had learned to write the characters with great neatness and celerity, so that he was of material use to me on this occasion; as he had been already before in transcribing the catalogue of the presents.
>
> (See *An Embassy to China; Lord Macartney's Journal 1793–1794*, edited by J. L. Cranmer-Byng. Longman's, 1962, pp. 99–100.)

After such an opening a word of explanation, if not of apology, may seem to be required, when offering the public no more than seventy-three short lyrics purporting to cover over a thousand years of writing in a specialized field of poetry.

Immensely popular with the Chinese, to whom music and poetry have always meant so much, the tz'u\* in the hands of some of the greatest poets was used for the expression of their liveliest and deepest feelings. This is exemplified by the 19 poems in the collection by Li Yü, one of the greatest writers of tz'u (page 29). Rather more colloquial than the traditional kind of poem—the 'shih'—and peculiarly well suited to the Chinese epigrammatic style, the tz'u has never received the same attention as the shih from the English translator.

Most Chinese lyrics possess a poignancy derived from an exuberant joy in living and a corresponding intensity of grief that youth and love and life itself are over so soon. The best are purged of sentimentality by their realism and acute power of observation. Man as an individual is as transitory as spring; but, unlike spring, he does not return. The splendour of ancient dynasties and the legendary heroes are gone; the rivers and the mountains they knew remain.

A 'Note on the Tz'u—its development and ornamentation', and Appendices (I-IV) are for readers who lack knowledge of Chinese poetry and would like a little more information about the circumstances under which the tz'u emerged and flourished. For those who know nothing about the way the poets lived, or the social and physical climate which influenced their outlook, that note will also serve to explain very briefly several allusions in the verses which might otherwise lose their point. The Appendix II (page 232) has more specific comment on points and allusions in the poems, particularly the historical verse, where explanation or even further translation seem necessary.

The Chinese have always regarded the visual ornamentation of a poem, the writing and arrangement of its characters, as an essential part of its enjoyment. There is a practical reason as well for facing each verse in English in this collection with the original in Chinese. During the hundreds of years which have intervened—and in some cases in this collection more than a thousand years—between the poet's work and today, it is not

---

\* The word 'tz'u' is pronounced enquiringly like a schoolboy's 'Sir?' with a 'T' in front, i.e. 'T'Sir'.

surprising that several differing versions of any one tz'u feature in separate anthologies; 'dawn' in one becomes 'evening' in another, 'a few' becomes 'myriads', and there are many wider differences still. The reader conversant with Chinese can at least see which edition has been used for the translation here.

Traditionally the Chinese have written out their tz'u without punctuation or otherwise marking the end of each line. As the tune-pattern was always noted the reader could find out, if he could not grasp it at once from the content of the poem, where succeeding lines began and ended. If an English reader wishes to compare the Chinese and English verse-patterns, reference may be made to Appendix III, where the numbers of characters in each line are given for each tune-pattern (p'u). The name of the p'u adopted for each poem is written immediately above each poem.

The Wade system of transliteration has been used to represent the Chinese sounds, except when the Chinese words, as for instance in Peking or Yangtze, are so well known that to use another form would appear pedantic or might be misleading. Appendix IV has been included to give the reader a simple guide to the pronunciation of those Chinese names occurring in the English poems.

Some earlier translators have presented Chinese poetry in a form too quaint to be impressive. Others, among them the greatest, have abandoned the use of rhyme, so marked and popular an ornamentation in Chinese poetry, especially so in the tz'u. In this small collection the object has been to reflect, as far as possible, the meaning, 'shape' (differing lengths and strengths of lines) and ornamentation of each lyric, in English verse that seeks to keep the Chinese spirit. Anyone who has seen the thumbed and dog-eared pages of a popular anthology of tz'u in Chinese hands, or has listened to the owner reciting his and the listener's favourites aloud, usually from memory, will understand the wish to try to pass on to English readers something of their fascination. If any such readers succeed in sharing the moods and feelings expressed in these poems to the extent that they are encouraged to look further, the book's purpose will have been served.

D.R.M.<br>A.F.G.A.

# ACKNOWLEDGEMENTS

MY THANKS ARE FIRSTLY DUE to C. K. Lam who introduced me, after several years away from the Chinese language, to the lyric and in particular to Li Yü's work, and who helped me in their interpretation. I owe a special debt of gratitude to Cheng Hsi for much help in translation; I look back with enormous pleasure to the many hours we spent together, which will remain memorable by his reciting and chanting of poetry, and his playing on the Chinese flute. Lee Yim has not only added greatly to this book by the harmonious elegance of his calligraphy (to be found opposite all the renderings into English except those illustrated) but was always ready to come to my aid with his wide experience and scholarship and has helped much over the selection of authoritative texts; and for this I am most grateful.

We are further indebted to Fei Ch'eng Wu and Chang Chien Ying, the former for his fine illustrations and the latter for her graceful calligraphy, which is to be found on the pages of her husband's work. Dr. Laurence Picken helped me over the piece of music attached to a poem by Ch'in Kuan, and Dr. K. P. K. Whitaker has been kind enough to advise me from time to time. T'ung Ping Cheng has revised Appendix III for me. Without these and other friends I could not have given to Alan Ayling the translations from which he could compose his verse.

To John Smith's skill and generosity in providing so much constructive criticism, creative help and encouragement we both owe a very special debt.

Eleven of the poems printed here have already appeared in the Poetry Review, to whose Editor we are grateful for permission to reprint.

D.R.M.

# T'ANG DYNASTY

# LI PO

(A.D. 701–762)

Li Po, one of the greatest of the T'ang Dynasty poets, was a man of tremendous personality. He had a reputation for improvising verses at any time on any subject, and particularly when he was full of wine. A confirmed Tao-ist, he believed in immortality and dabbled in alchemy. For some twenty years he wandered about from one place to another living as a recluse, or staying with relatives and friends, and sometimes doing an odd job of work.

For a brief period he was given a post attached to the Palace in Ch'ang-an in the Han Lin Academy, and stories are told of his becoming a special favourite of the Emperor. According to tradition the first lyric chosen for this collection was composed in honour of one of the Emperor's concubines (possibly, though this is disputed, the famous Yang Kuei Fei), and was set to music. But either because he had enemies at Court, or because he was found to be too irresponsible, or for both reasons, he only held the post for about three years and then resumed his peripatetic life.

He is renowned for the poetry he wrote in the traditional style, but the lyric (tz'u) was beginning to attract attention at this time and it is not surprising that Li Po was to be found in the forefront of the new form of verse; no doubt he was supremely confident that he could use it better than anyone else.

## 清平調　　　李白

雲想衣裳花想容春風拂檻露華濃

若非羣玉山頭見會向瑤臺月下逢

# 1

*P'u – Ch'ing P'ing Tiao*

Clouds bring back to mind her dress, the flowers her face.
Winds of spring caress the rail where sparkling dew-drops
    cluster.
If you cannot see her by the jewelled mountain top,
Maybe on the moonlit Jasper Terrace you will meet her.

## 憶秦娥

李白

簫聲咽秦娥夢橫秦樓月秦樓月年年柳色灞陵傷別

樂遊原上清秋節咸陽古道音塵絕音塵絕西風殘照漢家陵闕

# 2

*P'u – I Ch'in O*

    Sadly the flute notes bring
The heart of a girl with broken dreams in a moonlit
    tower of Ch'in,
    In a moonlit tower of Ch'in.
    Yearly the changing willows quicken
    Anguish of parting at Pa Ling.

It's Autumn Festival time once more on the heights of
    Lê-yu-yüan;
But the ancient road to Hsien-yang shows never a
    sign of him,
    Shows never a sign of him,
   A bleak wind stirs; declining rays
    Suffuse the imperial tombs of Han.

## 菩薩蠻　　李白

平林漠漠煙如織寒山一帶傷心碧暝色入高樓有人樓上愁　玉階空佇立宿鳥歸飛急何處是歸程長亭更短亭

# 3

*P'u – P'u Sa Man*

Clothed in mist the forest stretches, spreading deep and vast;
That green along the icy mountain range benumbs the breast.
      As gloomy night invades the storied tower
      The spirit droops in melancholy's power.

    Stand where the steps are bright as jade—how fast
      The birds fly over hastening back to roost!
      And will our own way home be hard to trace?
      At every stage there'll be a resting place.

## PO CHÜ I

### (A.D. 772–846)

Po Chü I, a native of Shensi province, passed the official literary examination for the doctorate of chin-shih with flying colours as the youngest student of his time. He later became a Director of the Han Lin Academy. His Government service follows the familiar pattern of promotion when a protector was in favour in Court, and dismissal and temporary banishment when the protector had to give way to a hostile successor. He served as Governor of both the important cities of Hangchow (822) and Soochow (825).

Po Chü I earned during his lifetime a unique esteem and popularity among his contemporaries of all classes based on his poetry written in the traditional style and including several long romantic poems. His work is particularly clear and comparatively free from the allusions and ambiguities common among Chinese poets. The two tz'u in this collection are included to indicate, as do those of Li Po, the early development of this new medium of expression.

## 花非花

白居易

花非花霧非霧夜半來天明去來如
春夢幾多時去似朝雲無覓處

# 4

*P'u – Hua Fei Hua*

A flower and not a flower; of mist yet not of mist;
At midnight she was there; she went as daylight shone.
She came and for a little while was like a dream of spring,
And then, as morning clouds that vanish traceless, she was gone.

長相思　　白居易

汴水流泗水流流到瓜洲古渡頭吳山點點愁

思悠悠恨悠悠恨到歸時方始休月明人倚樓

# 5

*P'u – Ch'ang Hsiang Ssu*

           Pien river flows;
           Ssu river flows.
Flowing on to Kua-chou's ancient ferry-point it goes.
Crest and crag, the peaks of Wu reflect another's woes.

           Brooding long and long;
           Grieving long and long,
Grieving till he comes again, for only then I'll stop.
The moon is bright; I, alone, lean from the turret-top.

# WEN T'ING YÜN
(about A.D. 820–870)

WEN T'ING YÜN was the first poet to specialize in the technique of the tz'u, shaping the pattern of his lines exactly to fit the music of the popular songs being sung at the time. A great number of his lyrics have come down to us in the collection known as the Hua Chien Chi. He spent a lot of his time enjoying the night life of the T'ang capital (Ch'ang-an) in the company of singing girls. He earned a reputation for his speed in composing poetry; he was nick-named 'Eight Clasp Wen' because, by the time he had clasped his hand eight times, he had written eight lines of verse. But while he maintained a skilful technical mastery of the lyric, his verses are without great depth, and one twentieth-century Chinese scholar used a line of the poem which follows to characterize his writings as 'the painting of a golden bird'.

## 更漏子

温庭筠

柳丝长春雨细花外漏声迢递惊塞雁起城乌画屏金鹧鸪 香雾薄透帘幕惆怅谢家池阁红烛背绣帘垂梦长君不知

# 6

*P'u – Keng Lou Tzu*

Long silk willow branches,
Fine spring rain.
Beyond the flowers a water-clock drips on, remote but plain.
A skein of flighting geese
Awakes the city crows—
Gold on the painted screen a partridge glows.

Fingers of scented mist
Between the curtains twist;
Sadly there returns to mind the Hsieh domain of years ago.
Behind the scarlet candles
Falls an embroidered screen.
My dream is long; a dream you do not know.

# FIVE DYNASTIES

## NAN T'ANG CHUNG CHU
## LI YING\*
(A.D. 916–961)

Li Ying was the second of the three sovereigns of the Southern T'ang Dynasty, and lived in a period of China's history referred to generally as the Five Dynasties (Wu Tai), between the break-up of the unified empire of the T'ang Dynasty and re-unification under the Sungs. He appears to have been an outstanding man both as an administrator, scholar and poet; at the age of ten he was already writing verse.

In A.D. 961 Li Ying, who was till then an independent sovereign, threw in his lot with the powerful Chao K'uang Yin (Sung T'ai Tsu), the founder of the Sung Dynasty in the north. After his submission as a vassal of the Sungs, he must have looked back with nostalgia to his days of complete freedom; indeed nostalgia permeates both poems in this collection and in particular may explain the reference in the second poem (line 5) to the Cock Fort (see Appendix II, p. 233). He seems to have been much more skilful in handling the Sungs than was his son Li Yü, the last of the Nan T'ang rulers (see page 29).

\* We appreciate that this ruler is usually referred to as Li Ching, but decided to use the name Li Ying, as preferred by some Chinese.

## 浣溪沙　　李　璟

手捲真珠上玉鉤依前春恨鎖重樓風裏落花誰是主思悠悠　青鳥不傳雲外信丁香空結兩中愁回首綠波三楚暮接天流

# 7

*P'u – T'an P'o Wan Ch'i Sha*

Now, as my hand rolls up the blind to reach its hook of jade,
Sorrow for spring again assails me in my cloistered shade.
Who is the master once the wind-blown blossom's fallen free?
        I wonder anxiously.

The orioles bring no messages from cloudland's distant groves.
My troubles grow entwined as rain-drenched blossom on the
    cloves.
Green billows in the three ravines I watch as day goes by
        Press on to reach the sky.

## 又　　　李璟

菡萏香銷翠葉殘　西風愁起綠波間　還與容光共憔悴不堪看　細雨夢回雞塞遠　小樓吹徹玉笙寒　多少淚珠何限恨倚闌干

# 8

*P'u – T'an P'o Wan Ch'i Sha*

Dead now the water-lily's scent, kingfisher gloss of leaf.
Across green waves to the lake-side the west wind ferries grief.
I who shared spring's glory share in autumn life's decay.
              Appalled, I turn away.

The distant Cock Fort fills my dream; I wake to a fine rain.
Sheng notes sound from the small pavilion, cold yet sweet their
    strain.
Tears, so many tears; what end to grief? I wonder, leaning
              Disconsolate on the railing.

# NAN T'ANG HOU CHU (LI YÜ)
## (A.D. 937–978)

Li Yü was the sixth son of Li Ying, and the last of three sovereigns of the Southern T'ang Dynasty. He was born in A.D. 937, came to the throne on his father's death in 961, and died in 978 after having been taken into captivity by the Sungs to Pien-liang (the city now known as K'ai-feng).

Li Yü was a scholar, poet, musician and painter—but not an administrator; the Sung Emperor T'ai Tsu is reported to have said, 'If Li Yü had been as skilful in ruling his country as in writing poems, how could I have ever captured him?' The easy life he led before his capture softened him. After the death of his first Queen he married her younger sister, but he had already been dallying with the younger one (see poem, p. 39) while the Queen was on a bed of sickness. In his pre-captivity tz'u his sensitive observation combines with a zest for living and single-minded pursuit of his own desires, dangerously irresponsible in a king. He is said to have been busy composing verses while his capital was falling: his poem (see Poem 27) describing his farewell to the Palace is very revealing.

He was then, in A.D. 975, taken into captivity, and died three years later having been poisoned, so it is said, by the order of Sung T'ai Tsu's successor and younger brother T'ai Tsung. The story is that T'ai Tsung suspected one of Li Yü's poems, which must have had a very ready audience, of carrying some hidden message of incitement to rebellion (see Poem No. 25, line 3).

It was during this period of captivity that his poems acquired an edge and poignancy which has led them to be quoted throughout the centuries up till this day. His style, brilliant in the use of simple words, in the ability to make most effective use of the juxtaposition of the long and short lines of the tunes to which he wrote his lyrics, and with a complete lack of classical allusion, is held to be, almost uniquely, beyond imitation. This is a formidable claim in a field of literature where most aspiring scholars and poets regarded copying, imitating and taking off the works of others as a pastime.

In this collection Poems Nos. 9–16 are assumed to be those written in his pre-captivity days, and Nos. 17–27 while he was a captive.

## 望江梅　　李煜

閒夢遠南國正芳春船上管絃江面綠滿城飛絮滾輕塵忙殺看花人

閒夢遠南國正清秋千里江山寒色遠蘆花深處泊孤舟笛在月明樓

# 9

*P'u – Wang Chiang Mei*

        Idle dreams of the far away
    Land of the south just as it blooms in spring.
A boat alive with music on the river running green;
  The city full of willow-down and dust upon the wing,
        And anxious eyes that watch earth's blossoming.

        Idle dreams of the far away
    Land of the south just at clear autumn light.
Endless miles of hill and river cold and remote in colour;
  Deep in the tufted rushes moored, a solitary boat;
    And from the moonlit turret top, a flute.

## 一斛珠　　李煜

曉妝初過沈檀輕注些兒箇向人微露丁香顆一曲清歌暫引櫻桃破　羅袖裛殘殷色可杯深旋被香醪涴繡床斜凭嬌無那爛嚼紅茸笑向檀郎唾

# 10

*P'u – I Ho Chu*

        Her morning toilet done she stood
    And in the censer lightly sprinkled sandalwood.
Then, with a glimpse of pearly teeth she turns her head
      Towards him, singing sweet and clear
          From lips of cherry red.

Stains on her silken sleeve rich depths of colour spread
    From cups filled and refilled with fragrant wine.
      Provocative, with careless grace
          she leans across the embroidered bed,
      Chews at a scrap of scarlet wool,
    Smiles, and then spits it in her lover's face.

## 搗練子令  李煜

深院靜小庭空斷續寒砧斷續風無奈夜長人不寐數聲和月到簾櫳

# 11

*P'u – Tao Lien Tzu Chin*

      Deep garden, calm and still;
      Bare arbour, sought by none;
Come and go of gusts and chill slap of sodden cloth on stone.
    Sad it is that all night long some lie awake alone.
The sounds that reach my lattice now come floating on the moon.

## 菩薩蠻　　　李煜

銅簧韻脆鏘寒竹　新聲慢奏移纖玉　眼色暗相鉤　秋波橫欲流　　雨雲深繡戶　未便諧衷素　讌罷又成空　夢迷春雨中

# 12

*P'u – P'u Sa Man*

Frailly through the metal reed, vibrant in the cold bamboo
   Slender fingers frame a style of music slow and new.
     With secret looks they tempt each other so,
    At once the waves of longing yearn to flow.

With rain and cloud behind the embroidered door
   Comes harmony the heart has hungered for.
     After the feasting emptiness again:
    Then dreams confused, that merge with the spring rain.

又　　　李煜

花明月暗籠輕霧，今朝好向郎邊去。刬襪步香堦，手提金縷鞋。　畫堂南畔見，一向偎人顫。奴為出來難，教君恣意憐。

# 13

*P'u – P'u Sa Man*

Glimmer of flowers, a shrouded moon and shallow mist for cover;
A perfect moment this to steal away and join her lover.
        Down scented paths in stockinged feet she goes,
        Clasped in her hands her gold-embroidered shoes.

        The south side of the painted hall their tryst;
        She leans one instant quivering on his breast:
        'So seldom can I come to you, my love,
        That all the love you ask of me, I give!'

## 喜遷鶯　　　李煜

曉月墮宿雲微無語枕頻欹夢回芳草思依依天遠雁聲稀　啼鶯散餘花亂寂寞畫堂深院片紅休掃儘從伊留待舞人歸

# 14

*P'u – Hsi Ch'ien Ying*

The dawn moon is setting,
The night-mist wearing thin;
Silent on my pillow I toss and sleep again.
My dreams are all of fragrant plants that cling to life they love.
Wild geese are calling high above.

As orioles pipe and scatter
The shaken blossoms fall.
It's lonely by the sunken court in the painted hall.
Don't sweep up the scarlet petals, leave them lying at their best
For the dancers coming late to their rest.

## 玉樓春　　　李煜

晚妝初了明肌雪春殿嬪娥魚貫列笙簫吹斷水雲間重按霓裳歌遍徹　臨春誰更飄香屑醉拍闌干情味切歸時休照燭花紅待放馬蹄清夜月

# 15

*P'u – Yü Lou Ch'un*

Evening adornment over now, their skin like shining snow,
At the Spring Hall the Palace beauties wind in heel to toe.
The flute that lulled to rest those liquid notes that float and flow
Rouses again, and now we sing the 'Rainbow Skirt' right through.

From whom, I wonder, does the wind that scent of powder blow?
Enriched with wine we beat the rail in rhythm—and still we glow!
When we return I'll have no candles lit for shine or show;
Riding my horse under the clear light of the moon I'll go.

## 臨江仙　　李煜

櫻桃落盡春歸去　蝶翻金粉雙飛　子規啼月小樓西　畫簾珠箔　惆悵捲金泥

門巷寂寥人去後　望殘煙草低迷

# 16

*P'u – Lin Chiang Hsien*

The cherry's bloom has wasted from the tree; the spring is gone.
    Butterflies in pairs flutter their powdered wings.
    At moonrise a night-jar calls from the west pavilion.
    I roll the beaded golden-spangled curtains
        Aside as melancholy weighs me down.

Now that the guests have found their way and gone, how still
    the lane!
    Mist low on the grass softens the horizon.
    Incense rising from the stove drifts idly up to heaven.
    Pondering, I smooth my silken girdle.
        Turning away I mourn the past, alone.

多少恨昨夜
夢魂中還似
舊時遊上苑
車如流水馬
如龍花月正
春風 　望江南
　　　李煜

# 17

*P'u – Wang Chiang Nan*

        No end to pain!
Last night in dreams—where still I reign—
My spirit wandered, as in old times, over my domain.
Carriages flowed like water and horses like a dragon.
    Flowers and the moon greeted spring winds again.

## 烏夜啼　　李煜

林花謝了春紅，太怱怱，無奈朝來寒雨晚來風。

臙脂淚，留人醉，幾時重，自是人生長恨水長東。

# 18

*P'u - Wu Yeh T'i*

    The sap of spring has ebbed, its flush of pride
        Too quickly died:
How else, when bitter morning rain and storm at night preside.
      A powdered tear-wet face,
      A man's enraptured gaze—
    Will these come back, the long-denied?
Rivers flow east for ever; life and suffering abide.

烏夜啼　　李煜

無言獨上西樓月如鉤寂寞梧桐深院鎖清秋
翦不斷理還亂是離愁別是一般滋味在心頭

# 19

*P'u – Wu Yeh T'i*

Solitary, mute, to the western tower I go.
The moon's a bow.
Autumn is locked in the garden's depths where the phoenix
branches grow.
Cut and cut, it will not sever;
Loosen, it's entwined as ever;
This is separation's woe.
It leaves the heart with a stain, the bruise of its blow.

浣溪沙　　　　李煜

轉燭飄蓬一夢歸欲尋陳跡悵人非天教心願與身違待月池臺空逝水映花樓閣漫斜暉登臨不惜更霑衣

# 20

*P'u – Wan Ch'i Sha*

Aimless, adrift in time, I dreamed that I returned. In vain
Seeking old haunts, I found the faces changed and felt the pain.
My every wish denied, their stark reverse the heavens ordain.

Terrace and lake, for moonlit parties planned, like water spilt
Had gone. On flower and palace shone immense the sunset mane.
I climbed and gazed and had no thought for tear-wet sleeves
    again.

## 子夜歌　　　李煜

人生愁恨何能免銷魂獨我情何限故國夢重
歸覺來雙淚垂高樓誰與上長記秋晴望往事
已成空還如一夢中

# 21

*P'u – Tzu Yeh Ko*

How can a man be free from sorrow in this mortal life?
Alone and broken-hearted, overwhelmed with endless grief,
      In dreams I am taken to my old country
      And wake to find a tear-drop in each eye.

    Who's here to climb the tower with me and gaze
        Afar, as once on perfect autumn days?
    Old days that time has emptied so, they seem
    Like fragments from a still unfinished dream.

## 清平樂　　　李煜

別來春半　觸目愁腸斷　砌下落梅如雪亂　拂了一身還滿

雁來音信無憑　路遙歸夢難成　離恨恰如春草　更行更遠還生

# 22

*P'u – Ch'ing P'ing Le*

  Since I left spring's half gone by.
   All I look at feeds my misery.
 Down garden steps plum blossom petals fall, in snow-drifts lie;
  You brush them off and still its snow you're covered by.

The wild geese have flown in yet there's no trace of news.
 The journey is too long even in dreams to dare.
 The bitter grief of leaving is like the spring grass;
  However far you go you find it growing there.

浪淘沙令　　　　李煜

簾外雨潺潺春意闌珊羅衾不耐五更寒夢裏不知身是客一晌貪歡

獨自莫憑闌無限江山別時容易見時難流水落花春去也天上人間

# 23

*P'u – Lang T'ao Sha*

    Outside the lattice rain-drops ring and bring
        The transient loveliness of spring.
No silken quilt withstands the cold of dawn's awakening.
Deep in my dreams just now I did not feel my captive state:
        I was happy—as a king.

    At lonely dusk I lean on the railing
        With visions of that boundless land.
To leave is easy, yes; but hard, how hard re-entering.
The water flows, the flowers wither, spring has passed me by.
        Earth is low; heaven, high.

## 浪淘沙　　　　李煜

往事只堪哀，對景難排，秋風庭院蘚
侵階，一桁珠簾閒不卷，終日誰來。

金劍已沈埋，壯氣蒿萊，晚涼天靜月
華開，想得玉樓瑤殿影，空照秦淮。

# 24

*P'u – Lang T'ao Sha*

    Grief rules the past—hard to forget as I
      Look at the familiar scene, and sigh.
Autumn moans on the courtyard steps where creeping mosses
    lie;
    Filtering pearly light, a screen hangs idly down unrolled;
      Day long no visitor comes by.

    Battered and buried deep, my sword of gold:
      Ambition sprang, then learned to die.
    The night is cool and quiet, the moon rises in the sky.
      I picture the Jade Tower and Jasper Palace, their
        shadows
    Framed in silver on the Ch'in Huai.

## 虞美人　　　李煜

春花秋月何時了往事知多少小樓昨夜又東風故國不堪回首月明中　雕欄玉砌依然在只是朱顏改問君都有幾多愁恰似一江春水向東流

# 25

*P'u - Yü Mei Jen*

    Spring blossom, Autumn moon, when will they cease their come and go?
        Of all the past has meant, how much I know!
    Into this tower last night a wind swept out of the East again—
The old country! in the bright moonlight to taste that wind is too much pain.

    They must be shining still, the carved railing and jade inlay;
        We alone change and waste away.
    I ask you, how can I endure to feel such sadness grow?
My heart's a river flushed with spring that must for ever eastwards flow.

## 虞美人　　　李煜

風回小院庭蕪綠柳眼春相續憑闌半日獨無言依舊竹聲新月似當年　　笙歌未散尊前在池面冰初解燭明香暗畫堂深滿鬢清霜殘雪思難任

## 26

*P'u – Yü Mei Jen*

Wind aswirl in the small court, greenness of weed by the shelter
    And willow-catkins; changeless spring is here!
Leaning on the parapet, alone with silence half the day,
    Flute notes as of old I heard hailing the new moon;
    And the years fell away.

Music and singing enrapture still, wine-cup and bowl respond:
    The ice begins to melt across the pond:
Incense-clouded, candle-lit, the lofty painted hall is there . . .
    And here's my frosted head as white as fallen snow.
    Such thought is hard to bear.

破陣子　　　李煜

四十年來家國三千里地山河鳳閣龍樓連霄漢玉樹瓊枝作烟蘿幾曾識干戈　一旦歸

為臣虜沈腰潘鬢消磨最是倉皇辭廟日教坊猶奏別離歌垂淚對宮娥

# 27

*P'u – P'o Chen Tzu*

During the forty years at home in my country,
Its three thousand miles of mountain-side and river,
Where Phoenix Hall and Dragon Tower touch the Milky Way
And jade trees with coral branches spread their misty cover,
When did I think of spear and buckler? Never!

Then one day I found myself a captive, a slave;
A back like Shen's and hair like P'an's my hardships tell.
The time I suffered most was setting out to leave the
   Temple:
The royal band still played a lamentation in farewell;
Facing the palace women, the tears fell.

# SUNG
# DYNASTY

## FAN CHUNG YEN
### (A.D. 989–1052)

As well as being a good poet Fan Chung Yen is an outstanding example of the best of government servants selected through the strictly classical examination system. He became a civil governor, military leader and finally rose to the position of Grand Councillor. Starting in life in straitened circumstances he passed his chin-shih doctorate, and then rose from acting mayor in the capital to Governor of Jao-chow. From there he was appointed as Military Governor in the west to defend the frontier against Tartar tribes and it is as a result of this period that he wrote with such feeling of the lonely conditions on the border (see p. 73). The enemy as well as the local tribes there were said to have had a great respect for him, and the Bactrians against whom he was fighting are said to have applied to him the phrase, 'Fan Chung Yen had myriads of armed soldiers in his breast.'* His name comes down to us as a man of great intelligence, a disciplinarian and a student of human nature. There are stories of his generosity to the poor on his estate to whom he granted land and of his kindly nature; his reply to his bailiff, who had explained a heavy loss of rent (collected in grain) as due to the depredations of birds and rats, was simply, 'Ah, what magnificent birds, what tremendous rats.'

It says something of Fan Chung Yen too that his son Fan Ch'un Jen (Yao Fu) is also remembered as a charitable sympathetic man.

* See Stewart Lockhart, *A Manual of Chinese Quotations*.

## 漁家傲　　范仲淹

塞下秋來風景異衡陽雁去無留意
四面邊聲連角起千嶂裏長煙落日
孤城閉濁酒一杯家萬里燕然未
勒歸無計羌管悠悠霜滿地人不寐
將軍白髮征夫淚

# 28

*P'u – Yü Chia Ao*

As autumn invades the frontier lands nature's pattern changes.
With never a thought to linger here the geese fly south and past;
While all around rough border songs ring out and horns resound.
            Among peak-studded ranges
Light dies in misty coils; forlorn, the city gate shuts fast.

      A glass of muddy wine to home a thousand miles away!
    We have gained no glory here; the only plan, to stay.
Far distant sound the tribal pipes; black frost has gripped the
                ground
            And nobody can sleep.
Your general's hair is white: in the darkness the soldiers weep.

## 蘇幕遮

范仲淹

碧雲天黃葉地秋色連波波上寒煙翠山映斜陽天接水芳草無情更在斜陽外　黯鄉魂追旅思夜夜除非好夢留人睡明月樓高休獨倚酒入愁腸化作相思淚

# 29

*P'u – Su Mu Che*

>Blue in a cloud-swept sky;
On earth the yellowing leaves
Bring Autumn to the river's edge
Where emerald vapour cloaks the waves.
Hills brighten in the setting sun as sky and river merge below.
The care-free grasses spring and spread
To lands beyond the sunset glow.

>Heavy and sick for home
I scan my travelled past;
Night after night, only when dreams
Were good, I fell asleep at last.
It is not wise to lean alone in the high tower when moonlight stirs;
The wine will make your torment worse
And turn too soon to home-sick tears.

## 御街行　　范仲淹

紛紛墜葉飄香砌　夜寂靜寒聲碎　真珠簾捲玉樓空　天淡銀河垂地　年年今夜　月華如練　長是人千里

愁腸已斷無由醉　酒未到先成淚　殘燈明滅枕頭敧　諳盡孤眠滋味　都來此事　眉間心上　無計相迴避

## 30

*P'u - Yü Chieh Hsing*

A mass of fallen leaves is drifting down each scented step.
        Deep in the silent night
        The cold cracks like a whip.
The pearly blind's rolled up; there's no one in the House of Jade.
     A moonstone sky, the Milky Way descending; year
        By year to greet this night's return
        The moonbeams fall like shining silk.
       My lover waits a thousand miles from here.

Now that my grief has broken me the urge to drink is dead;
        The wine remains untouched,
        I taste my tears instead.
As the dying lamplight wavers I rest my pillowed head;
  I know too well the sleep they find who lie alone.
        When all these thoughts rise up as one
        And brows bend with the heart's burden
       There's no retreat, no way around them, none.

# YEH CH'ING CH'EN
## (?)

YEH CH'ING CH'EN was an eleventh-century poet; he took his chin-shih doctorate in 1024. After government service in Chekiang province, where he was concerned chiefly with water transportation and regulation work, in which he distinguished himself to the good of the public, he was appointed to the Han Lin Academy at the capital.

So bald a description of so 'worthy' a person does not prepare the reader for the robust flavour of the single tz'u that follows.

## 賀聖朝 葉清臣

滿斟綠醑留君住莫怱怱歸去三分春色二分愁更一分風雨　花開花謝都來幾許且高歌休訴不知來歲牡丹時再相逢何處

# 31

*P'u - Ho Sheng Chao*

Fill up your glasses with crystal green wine and stay!
Don't make a stir about going away!
Spring has three essences, two give us grief and pain—
Yes, and the third one is tempest and rain!
Flowers bloom, flowers die—
All the time, endlessly!
Cheer up, then, this is no time to complain!
Next year, at paeony blossom time who can say
Where we'll foregather again?

# YEN SHU
## (A.D. 991–1055)

YEN SHU was composing verse at the age of seven, and was reported to the Throne later as a budding genius. The story is told that when he went to compete in the official examination at Court for the chin-shih doctorate qualification he found the examination paper contained the very question which he had recently been studying deeply. He reported this as a fact which would give him an unfair advantage and asked for another subject on which to write his essay. This does not seem to have affected the result and he emerged successful.

Yen Shu was a man of a relaxed and peaceful disposition, and was well known as a writer of tz'u. One of the two examples of his work included here (see p. 85) is sometimes attributed to Nan T'ang Chung Chu (Li Ying).

浣溪沙　　　晏殊

一曲新詞酒一杯去年天氣舊亭臺夕陽西下幾時迴　無可奈何花落去似曾相識燕歸來小園香徑獨徘徊

# 32

*P'u – Wan Ch'i Sha*

One new poem and a glass of wine to make it flow!
At the old pavilion last year's weather's all we know.
The sun dwindles in the west—when will it start to grow?

Nothing can restore the blossom once it falls in snow . . .
Yet, almost, I recognize each incoming swallow.
Alone on scented garden paths I wander to and fro.

## 破陣子　　　晏殊

燕子來時新社　梨花落後清明　池上碧苔三四點　葉底黃鸝一兩聲　日長飛絮輕

巧笑東鄰女伴　采桑徑裏逢迎　疑怪昨宵春夢好　元是今朝鬥草贏　笑從雙臉生

# 33

*P'u – P'o Chen Tzu*

With the swallow comes the time for the village festival,
And it's Ch'ing Ming time as soon as the pear-blossom dies.
There are still only three or four patches of duck-weed on the pond
And behind the leaves the golden oriole pipes only once or twice.
      Days lengthen, willow-down flies.

The girl from my neighbour's house to the east gathering
Mulberry leaves, meets me and smiling confidingly says
'I was wondering why I was sent such a happy spring dream last night,
And now I know, in the grass-game this morning I took the first place!'
      Her smile spread over her face.

# YEN CHI TAO
## (?)

YEN CHI TAO was the youngest son of Yen Shu (see p. 83). He seems to have failed in official life and to have devoted himself to poetry, but poverty made him an unhappy person and his verse misses the relaxed quality of his father's.

There is a story behind the poem included here that during his father's life-time, when Yen Chi Tao was living in the family mansion, he fell in love with one of the girls of the household—Hsiao P'in (see page 236). The liaison would not have been encouraged, and when the father died and the money ran out the household staff had to be dispersed. A year after his last sight of her, Yen Chi Tao, waking up after a late night, is reminded of her presence among the flowers of last year's spring, while swallows—symbols of happily married people—fly in the fine rain.

## 臨江仙　　晏幾道

夢後樓臺高鎖　酒醒簾幕低垂　去年春恨卻來時　落花人獨立　微雨燕雙飛

記得小蘋初見　兩重心字羅衣　琵琶絃上說相思　當時明月在　曾照彩雲歸

# 34

*P'u – Lin Chiang Hsien*

    After my dream I woke in the tall tower, withdrawn.
      My mind had cleared; the curtain still hung down.
Spring with its last year's grief was with me once again:
        There she had trod the fallen flowers, alone,
      While pairs of swallows flew in the fine rain.

    I remember the first time I set eyes on her:
'Heart' had been embroidered on both the silks she wore;
The strings of her guitar sang of the thoughts we shared.
      The moon that shone so bright, that's still up there,
        Made rainbows of her dress as she appeared.

# OU YANG HSIU
(A.D. 1007–1072)

OU YANG HSIU was a man of learning and uprightness, who rose from a home of poverty—his mother taught him to write with a reed, not having enough money to buy a proper brush—to the highest political positions. He was acknowledged as a great writer of prose and verse, a historian, and essayist.

Doubt has been thrown on the authenticity of some of his lyrics in that as a devout Confucian he would not have written love-poetry. However, there is at least one story told about him which would tend to support the inclusion in anthologies of the tz'u (printed in this collection) under his name. A local official about to receive a visit from Ou Yang Hsiu told the singing-girl, who was to appear as light entertainment, to prepare to sing lyrics (tz'u) in his honour. At the dinner Ou Yang Hsiu seemed to be listening to the singing with unusual attention and to be thoroughly enjoying himself with the wine. This somewhat surprised his host until he learnt from the girl afterwards that she had sung nothing but Ou Yang Hsiu's own tz'u.

生查子　　　歐陽修

去年元夜時花市燈如畫月上柳梢頭人約黃昏後　今年元夜時月與燈依舊不見去年人淚溼春衫袖

# 35

*P'u – Sheng Ch'a Tzu*

> At last year's Lantern Festival
> The flower market was bright as day.
> The moon had climbed the willow tops.
> At twilight end he came my way.
>
> At this year's Lantern Festival
> Moonlight and lamplight shine no less.
> I have not seen my last year's love.
> Tears wet the sleeves of my spring dress.

浣溪沙　　　　歐陽修

堤上遊人逐畫船拍堤春水四垂天綠楊樓外出鞦韆　　白髮戴花君莫笑六么催拍盞頻傳人生何處似尊前

# 36

*P'u – Wan Ch'i Sha*

Strollers on the river-side are following the pleasure-boats
Where spring-tide waters lap the banks under a tented sky.
Willows frame in green a tower and jutting outline of a swing.

Do not laugh because a flower is hanging from this hair so white;
But think, as the 'Lu Yao's' restless beat urges the toasts around,
Has life a place can match with this in front of a cup of wine?

## 訴衷情

歐陽修

清晨簾幕捲輕霜　呵手試梅妝　都緣自有離恨　故畫作遠山長

思往事　惜流光　易成傷　未歌先歛　欲笑還顰　最斷人腸

# 37

*P'u – Su Chung Ch'ing*

The blinds, still lightly frosted, are rolled up at break of day.
    Deftly she tries the 'Plum' style hair display;
Then, overwhelmed by grief because he's gone, she paints
    Her eye-brows like that line of long hills far away.

    Thinking of other days,
    Saddened that time goes by,
    How natural to feel injury!
    And so the song was never sung,
    The smile lay still-born in her frown:
    Heartbreak and agony.

南歌子　　歐陽修

鳳髻金泥帶龍紋玉掌梳走來窗下笑相扶愛道畫眉深淺入時無　弄筆偎人久描花試手初等閒妨了繡工夫笑問雙鴛鴦字怎生書

## 38

*P'u - Nan Ko Tzu*

        Hair dressed in phoenix style, ribbon dipped in gold,
            With figures of dragons her jade comb chased.
Smiling, gay, they greeted each other as up to the window he paced.
She wanted to ask if her eye-brown pencilling followed fashion's taste.

        Long she dallies with him as she works her brush;
          At first she tries her hand at painting a flower,
Idles away her time for needlework; then, smilingly, 'Sir,
A Mandarin drake and duck,' she asks, 'how do I write each character?'

臨江仙　　　　歐陽修

柳外輕雷池上雨　雨聲滴碎荷聲　小樓西角斷
虹明　闌干倚處　待得月華生　　燕子飛來窺
畫棟　玉鈎垂下簾旌　涼波不動簟紋平　水精雙
枕傍　有墮釵橫

## 39

*P'u – Lin Chiang Hsien*

Far thunder beyond the willows; on the lake rain is falling,
    Drops drum down on every floating lily pad.
From the west side of the small house, look, a bright broken rainbow,
    As I lean upon the railing
    Waiting for the moon to raise its head.

Swallows, hawking round the painted pillars, flicker, dip and flow;
    Now the jade hook lets the unlooped curtain go.
Cooling waves of air against the bamboo blinds no ripple show.
    Two bright pillows on the bed;
    By their side, a golden hair-pin shed.

## 蝶戀花

歐陽修

庭院深深深幾許楊柳堆烟簾幕無重數玉勒雕鞍游冶處樓高不見章臺路　雨橫風狂三月暮門掩黃昏無計留春住淚眼問花花不語亂紅飛過秋千去

# 40

*P'u – Tieh Lien Hua*

      Deep, deep, how deep my courtyard lay,
        Mist in swathes among the willows.
    To countless curtained doors the rich and gay,
With bridles of jade and saddles subtly carved, for pleasure stray.
      My turret overlooked no such Pavilion of Display.

Driving rain, tempestuous wind make an end of spring's array.
        The twilight dims on shuttered doors.
    Who knows what spell might charm the spring to stay?
With tear-filled eyes we ask the flowers, the flowers will not say,
   For the blossom was blown flying over the swing and away.

# LIU YUNG
## (about A.D. 1045)

LIU YUNG had the chance of going into government circles but preferred a free and easy life spending much of his time in the courtesan quarter. Anyone so intelligent was bound to be considered as a recruit for government service, but hearing how the poet lived the Emperor is said to have remarked, 'Let him go on writing poetry.' This gave Liu Yung the excuse to claim thereafter that he was 'following the Emperor's instruction to compose tz'u'.

He can be said to have given a new turn to this form of poetry. From the typical tz'u of his in this collection it will be seen first that its length (over 100 characters) is double, or more than double, that of the earlier tz'u (of about 25–50 characters). This lengthening of the tz'u meant that the picture quickly drawn with a few brush strokes and with the minimum of linking between one stroke and another—exemplified by Wen T'ing Yün's style—was expanded by Liu Yung into a more complex composition. Liu Yung works out his theme in greater detail and without the economy of language used by the earlier writers of tz'u. Furthermore, writing so much for the singing girls, he tended even more than his predecessors to develop a colloquial style.

His sensitive love lyrics were immensely popular, and a visiting envoy to China is said to have remarked, 'Wherever there is a well, someone will be singing Liu Yung's tz'u.'

## 雨霖鈴　　　柳永

寒蟬淒切對長亭晚驟雨初歇都門帳飲無緒留戀處蘭舟催發執手相看淚眼竟無語凝噎念去去千里煙波暮靄沈沈楚天闊　多情自古傷離別更那堪冷落清秋節今宵酒醒何處楊柳岸曉風殘月此去經年應是良辰好景虛設便縱有千種風情更與何人說

# 41

*P'u – Yü Lin Ling*

        The cold cicada's melancholy measure
    At evening fronts our shelter of farewell.
          The sudden savage rain is done.
Though wined and snug hard by the city, where's the pleasure?
          Just as we most need one another
          The boatmen urge me to be gone.
Then, hand in hand, we watch the tears brim in each other's eyes;
   Dumbly, in struggling throats our voices smother.
          I think of where I'm going,
        A thousand miles through mist and wave.
The night-haze cloaks a scene as vast as under Southern skies.

    Deeper natures know too well separation's misery.
    And how then shall I bear alone the autumn cold again?
    Tonight when I awake from too much wine where shall I be?
    By a willow-bank, a wind at dawn, the moon upon the wane.
       Tho' this time I'll be gone a year and more
Yet pleasant hours, enchanting scenes will cast their spell in vain!
        For even if my heart was stirred a thousand ways
            With whom could I discuss, to whom explain?

# SU SHIH

(A.D. 1036–1101)

Su Shih came of a very talented family. He rose to high position in government circles both in the capital and in the provinces, where he is specially known for his Governorship at Hangchow. But his success alternated with being out of favour and banishment, chiefly owing to his opposition to the great Sung reformer Wang An Shih. As a writer of poetry he is reckoned to be one of the three greatest in China. His critics accused him of using the lyric form—tz'u—as simply another way of exploiting his own style and idioms instead of working within previously accepted limitations as to subject-matter and song-pattern. His talent and vigour brought new life to the lyric, which otherwise, under the influence of the sentimental school of Liu Yung and others, would almost certainly have decayed into pretty exercises of skill.

Su Shih is said to have asked a friend how he thought Liu Yung's tz'u compared with his own. 'Liu Yung's tz'u,' said the friend, 'suit a teen-age girl with a red ivory clapper singing: "By a willow bank, a wind at dawn, the moon upon the wane" (see Poem 41). While yours need a great big fellow from the wild border country with a bronze guitar and an iron clapper to sing: "The great river surges east"' (see Poem 46).

The 'Ode to the Red Cliff' (see Poem 46) was written about 1083 when he was under a form of 'open arrest'—that is out of favour, banished from Court, but allowed to live a life of his own provided he did not stir from a prescribed area. His great theme was the transitoriness of man and all his glories compared with the never-changing rhythm of nature's cycle. It was at this time that he became a farmer and called himself the Recluse of the Eastern Slope (Tung P'o) and it is from this place-name that he is familiarly known as Su Tung P'o. At his retreat he was supremely happy, looking down from the hills to 'the great river'—the Yangtze.

## 卜算子 　　蘇軾

水是眼波橫，山是眉峯聚。欲問行人去那邊，眉眼盈盈處。

才始送春歸，又送君歸去。若到江南趕上春，千萬和春住。

# 42

*P'u – Pu Suan Tzu*

    The river runs clear as the pool in your eye.
    Like eye-brows in arches the hills rise and mount.
    Ask where the traveller goes he will surely reply
        Where rivers and hills are too many to count.

    I am just over seeing the spring off: now
      It is you I see off to your home—and O,
If you manage to catch up the spring when you get to Chiang-
      nan,
    For heaven's sake cling to it, don't let it go!

卜算子　　　蘇軾

缺月挂疏桐漏斷人初靜誰見幽人獨往來縹
緲孤鴻影　　驚起卻回頭有恨無人省揀盡
寒枝不肯棲寂寞沙洲冷

# 43

*P'u – Pu Suan Tzu*

The young moon swings on a spray of the phoenix tree;
The water-clock's spent; quiet now is all that stirred;
Who will notice the recluse pacing about alone?
    Forlorn and shadowy gleams the shape of a bird;

    And now in fear it rises and turning its head
Looks back with mournful longing; nobody notices.
Closely it scans the cold branches, but scorning to rest in them
Seeks out in sandy flats a refuge comfortless.

## 洞仙歌　　　蘇軾

冰肌玉骨自清涼無汗水殿風來暗香滿繡簾開一點明月窺人人未寢欹枕釵橫鬢亂起來攜素手庭戶無聲時見疏星渡河漢試問夜如何夜已三更金波淡玉繩低轉但屈指西風幾時來又不道流年暗中偷換

## 44

*P'u – Tung Hsien Ko*

    Ice-smooth your skin, jade-smooth your bones;
      Cool and astringent, nature shaped you so.
  Thronging the Water Palace scented breezes blow.
        Between embroidered curtains
  A roving shaft of moonlight holds you in its stare.
        You're not asleep, you lie
Pillowed with tumbling hair-pin and dishevelled hair.

  Clasping your white hands close I raise you up.
      In court and hall no sound is heard:
  Stray meteors plunge in streaks across the Milky Way.
     You ask me how the night wears on: the third
        Watch is already with us now;
        The bright moon dims her ray,
    The Jade Rope Star is dipping low.
Just reckon on your fingers when the cool west wind's expected here:
We never guessed how stealthily the seasons would advance that day.

## 水調歌頭

蘇軾

明月幾時有把酒問青天不知天上宮闕今夕是何年我欲乘風歸去又恐瓊樓玉宇高處不勝寒起舞弄清影何似在人間　轉朱閣低綺戶照無眠不應有恨何事偏向別時圓人有悲歡離合月有陰晴圓缺此事古難全但願人長久千里共嬋娟

# 45

Su Shih prefaced this *Ode to the Autumn Moon* with a short note that he was thinking of his brother, and was inspired with wine.

*P'u – Shui Tiao Ko T'ou*

  Will a moon so bright ever arise again?
  Drink a cupful of wine and ask of the sky.
 I don't know where the palace gate of heaven is,
  Or even the year in which tonight slips by.
 I want to return riding the whirl-wind! But I
 Feel afraid that this heaven of jasper and jade
  Lets in the cold, its palaces rear so high.
 I shall get up and dance with my own shadow.
  From life endured among men how far a cry!

   Round the red pavilion
   Slanting through the lattices
   Onto every wakeful eye,
  Moon, why should you bear a grudge, O why
 Insist in time of separation so to fill the sky?
  Men know joy and sorrow, parting and reunion:
The moon lacks lustre, brightly shines; is all, is less.
  Perfection was never easily come by.
 Though miles apart, could men but live for ever
 Dreaming they shared this moonlight endlessly!

念奴嬌赤壁懷古　　蘇軾

大江東去浪淘盡千古風流人物故
壘西邊人道是三國周郎赤壁亂石
穿空驚濤拍岸捲起千堆雪江山如
畫一時多少豪傑　遙想公瑾當年
小喬初嫁了雄姿英發羽扇綸巾談
笑間檣櫓灰飛烟滅故國神遊多情
應笑我早生華髮人生如夢一尊還
酹江月

# 46

Ode to the Red Cliff

*P'u – Nien Nu Chiao*

>     The great river surges east.
>         Its waves have scoured away
>     Since time began all traces of heroic man.
>         The western side of the old fort
>             Was once, so people say,
>     Known as the Red Cliff of Chou of the Three Kingdoms.
>         With piled up rocks to stab the sky
>             And waves to shake them thunderously
>         Churning the frothy mass to mounds of snow,
>             It's like a masterpiece in paint.
>         Those ages hide how many a hero!
>
> Think back to those old days; that first year when Chou Yü
>     Had just been married to the Little Ch'iao.
>         Then, what a hero he became!
>             With waving fan and silken cap
>             He talked and laughed at ease
>     While masts and oars were blotted out in smoke and flame!
>         My wits that stray to realms of old
>             Deserve the scorn of all who feel;
>         Years pass, and hair grows white so soon.
>         Though a man's life is like a dream,
>     One toast continues still—the River and the Moon!

## 水龍吟

蘇軾

似花還似非花也無人惜從教墜拋家傍路思
量卻是無情有思縈損柔腸困酣嬌眼欲開還
閉夢隨風萬里尋郎去處又還被鶯呼起
不恨此花飛盡恨西園落紅難綴曉來雨過遺
蹤何在一池萍碎春色三分二分塵土一分流
水細看來不是楊花點點是離人淚

# 47

Ode to the Willow Flower

*P'u – Shui Lung Yin*

    Yes, it's a flower, but unlike any other flower.
  And no one spares a second thought upon it; let it go!
      Far from home, by the roadside strolling,
        I wonder about it; it looks as though
          It cannot feel, yet it must know;
      Around its heart the hairs twist so.
        Drowsy in sleep is its lovely eye;
    Though it would open them, shut the lids lie:
In dreams it follows the wind ten thousand miles
      To find where its companion fled.
Yet once again it rouses, stirred by the oriole's cry.

    It's not the willow flowers in flight that make me grieve:
I mourn the western garden blossom doomed beyond reprieve.
      Dawn is here and the rain is over;
        Where are the traces they should leave?
        The pond a mass of duck-weed drift!
        Of spring's gay-coloured triple gift
        Two parts are swallowed up in dust,
        The rest in downpour disappears!
And now look closely, these were never willow-flowers at all;
    The little drops you see are lovers' goodbye tears.

# HUANG T'ING CHIEN
## (A.D. 1045—1105)

POET and calligraphist of standing, he rose high in government service. Huang T'ing Chien was one of the four well-known students of Su Shih (another being Ch'in Kuan who follows in this collection of poems). He was best known as a writer of verse in the traditional style (shih). Though later criticism may have classed his tz'u as inferior to Ch'in Kuan's, nevertheless the two poems chosen here stand as good examples, and the second one (Poem 49) is particularly interesting for its rhyme and alliteration (see 'Note on the Tz'u', p. 225).

清平樂　　　　黃庭堅

春歸何處寂寞無行路若有人知春去處喚取歸來同住　春無蹤跡誰知除非問取黃鸝百轉無人能解因風飛過薔薇

# 48

*P'u – Ch'ing P'ing Le*

    Where has spring gone, where's he gone,
        Unaccompanied, all alone?
   If anyone knows, if anyone knows where spring has gone,
    Call him back to live with us as our companion.

Spring left no trace, no trace. The last chance now—who
    knows?—is
   From the oriole's mouth, although whatever she discloses—
     A myriad warbling notes nobody understands—
The wind, the wind will blow away over the red roses.

## 畫堂春　　　黃庭堅

東風吹柳日初長　雨餘芳草斜陽　杏花零落燕泥香　睡損紅妝

寶篆煙銷龍鳳　畫屏雲鎖瀟湘　夜寒微透薄羅裳　無限思量

# 49

*P'u - Hua T'ang Ch'un*

An east wind bends the willow-trees; days begin to lengthen;
 The rain is over; plants preen in the setting sun.
Scent of almond lingers in the swallows' nesting clay—
 Look how my sleep-smeared rouge has run!

Incense vapour curls in shapes of phoenix and of dragon;
 Clouds on the painted screen mantle the Hsiao and Hsiang.
Now the cold of night begins to pierce my filmy gown—
 Can thought know bounds, or are there none?

# CH'IN KUAN
## (A.D. 1049–1100)

THE FREQUENCY with which a clever poet would imitate another's work was well known and suitably borne in mind by critics. It was much more difficult to forge another man's writing. Ch'in Kuan is said to have written a poem on a monastery wall in Su Shih's style both of poetical composition and of calligraphy, and to have imitated Su Shih so well that the latter could not distinguish the result from his own writing. Su Shih then read some of Ch'in Kuan's work and recognized who the author of the piece on the monastery wall must be, later becoming good friends with him.

A Sung dynasty critic said of Ch'in Kuan:

> Su Shih's words are more beautiful than his feelings;
> Liu Yung's feelings are more beautiful than his words;
> The only one whose feelings match his words is Ch'in Kuan.

## 憶王孫　　　秦觀

萋萋芳草憶王孫柳外樓高空斷魂杜宇聲聲
不忍聞欲黃昏雨打梨花深閉門

## 50

*P'u – I Wang Sun*

The grass that grows so strongly there reminds me of my love
    As high above the willow in the turret-top I grieve.
    I cannot bear the churring of the night-jar any more;
        And now, at twilit eve,
Rain has struck the pear-blossom. Double lock each door!

## 滿庭芳　　秦觀

山抹微雲，天黏衰草，畫角聲斷譙門。暫停征棹，聊共引離尊。多少蓬萊舊事，空回首、煙靄紛紛。斜陽外，寒鴉數點，流水繞孤村。

銷魂，當此際，香囊暗解，羅帶輕分。謾贏得青樓薄倖名存。此去何時見也，襟袖上、空染啼痕。傷情處，高城望斷，燈火已黃昏。

# 51

*P'u – Man T'ing Fang*

        The mountain merges with the mist;
The sky-line's down to waning grass.
The watch-tower silences, the painted horn has ceased.
        The boat will not be leaving yet;
        This is the time to drink a farewell toast.
Enchanted hill, what memories of days gone by
        Our heads turn back to share!
        The evening mist is widely cast.
          Beyond the sun's slant rays
        A few crows huddle, black on white.
          A ring of water holds the village fast.

At this sad hour, with anguished grief oppressed,
        Shyly you steal your sachet free;
        Silk girdle loosed too easily!
I know myself for what I must appear, a heartless rake.
    And now we part: when can we hope to meet again?
Tears have fallen; on collar and sleeve they lie confessed.
        We touch the pitch of pain.
        From the high city walls your anxious eyes will see
Only the flickering lamps: night drowns the rest.

## CHOU PANG YEN
(A.D. 1057–1121)

CHOU PANG YEN was a musician and poet. Scholarship in recent years is revealing the intricacies of the melodic rhythm in his lyrics, complicated to the extent that he might well be classed as a maker of verbal jig-saw puzzles were it not for the beauty of the result. His poems were said to be 'as soft as pure cotton, but with a needle in the middle'.

His reasons for writing the first of the two tz'u selected are explained in the 'Note on the Tz'u' (p. 216). Briefly he was surprised by the Emperor, hid just in time, and wrote this all-too-faithful account of a preliminary exchange between the girl and the Emperor, which the latter recognized at once when he heard the verse repeated by some 'good friend'.

少年遊　　周邦彥

并刀如水吳鹽勝雪纖指破新橙錦

幄初溫獸香不斷相對坐調笙低

聲問向誰行宿城上已三更馬滑霜

濃不如休去直是少人行

## 52

*P'u – Shao Nien Yu*

> Knife from Ping as bright as water,
> Salt from Wu surpassing snow,
> An orange rare her slender fingers tear.
> Newly warmed embroidered curtains,
> Incense from the dragon burner;
> Playing the sheng they face each other there.
>
> Her low voice softly asks
> 'Where are you going to spend the night?
> They've called the third watch from the city wall.
> Your horse will slip, the frost's so thick;
> You'd do much better not to go;
> There's hardly anyone about at all.'

## 六醜　　　　周邦彥

正單衣試酒，悵客裏光陰虛擲。願春暫留春歸如過翼，一去無迹。為問家何在，夜來風雨，葬楚宮傾國。釵鈿墮處遺香澤，亂點桃蹊，輕翻柳陌。多情為誰追惜，但蜂媒蝶使時叩窗槅。

東園岑寂，漸蒙籠暗碧。靜繞珍叢底，成歎息。長條故惹行客，似牽衣待話，別情無極。殘英小強簪巾幘。終不似、一朶釵頭顫裊，向人欹側。漂流處，莫趁潮汐。恐斷紅尚有相思字，何由見得。

# 53

*P'u – Liu Ch'ou*                           Ode to a Red Rose

    Fresh changed in summer silks and sipping wine
And sick at heart; this time from home so emptily thrown away!
        If only spring would rest awhile!
     It fluttered by on bird's wings, would not stay:
        It left no trace, it stole away.
    And where's its home, you ask, and who can say!

      Wind and rain arose in the night
  And buried the matchless joy of the Ch'u Palace.
Fragrance lingers yet, as scent from a fallen hairpin may.
      Its petals strew the peach-bloom path,
       Whirled away where it skirts the willows.
Heart filled with longing! Who was there its anguish to allay?
     Only the bees and butterflies, those messengers,
      Fluttered about my window day by day.

    Withdrawn, remote, the eastern gardens lie.
  Though deepening green will cage them gradually,
        Now among sylvan beauties silently
          I walk alone, and sigh.
  Long spreading branches seem intent to block my way,
    Tug at my coat as if to catch what I may say . . .
      The pangs of separation quicken endlessly.
        With little fading blossoms
     I deck my hair: however hard I try
They're much too short to bend in grace like those that
          wave on pins
      Bowing as if to passers by.
You floating petals, drift no more though dawn and sunset tides
  run high;
It may be from the rose's heart you bear fond messages that still
        Elude my anxious eye.

# LI CH'ING CHAO
## (A.D. 1081–?)

LI CH'ING CHAO, a woman, came of a literary family and is known as China's greatest poetess. She is particularly famous for her tz'u, many of which reflect her deep feelings after the death of her husband.

## 醉花陰　　　李清照

薄暮濃雲愁永晝，瑞腦消金獸。佳節又重陽，玉枕紗廚，半夜涼初透。

東籬把酒黃昏後，有暗香盈袖。莫道不消魂，簾捲西風，人比黃花瘦。

## 54

*P'u – Tsui Hua Yin*

    Evening; the heavy cloud has seen the sad day through.
        Faintly the incense in the brazier burns.
        The enchanting Ch'ung Yang festival returns.
    Through screens of gauze on to her jade pillow
           Cool midnight airs begin to flow.

Down at the eastern hedge with wine at eve there'll be
        Unfathomable scents to fill her sleeves.
        But never doubt how bitterly she grieves;
    For when the west wind rolls the blind back, see,
          Frail as the yellow flowers is she.

# 聲聲慢

李清照

尋尋覓覓冷冷清清悽悽慘慘切切乍暖還寒時候最難將息三杯兩盞淡酒怎敵他晚來風急雁過也正傷心卻是舊時相識滿地黃花堆積憔悴損如今有誰堪摘守着窗兒獨自怎生得黑梧桐更兼細雨到黃昏點點滴滴這次第怎一個愁字了得

# 55

*P'u – Sheng Sheng Man*

        Unending search in endless quest
So cold and still, how cold and still;
By grief and anguish, grief and anguish hard oppressed.
   This season of the sudden change from warm to chill
     Weighs down the heart in search of peace.
       Cupfuls of light wine, two or three;
How else confront the wind that blows at dusk so urgently?
         Even the flighting geese
        Have stabbed me to the heart,
Friends that fly past me out of older memories.

Chrysanthemums in yellow masses everywhere:
    Melancholy has marked them for its own.
For whom are they worth gathering growing there?
    Watching from my window all alone
How am I to live until the darkness falls?
Fine rain is falling, too, into the wu t'ung trees;
Plodding drop by drop down into the dusk's uncertainties.
   Tell me, with this, then, with all this,
   How can the one word 'sorrow' paint what sorrow is?

# SOUTHERN SUNG
# DYNASTY

# YÜEH FEI
## (A.D. 1102–1141)

YÜEH FEI was a great and successful general of the Southern Sungs. The Nüchen Tartars had invaded China from the northeast, captured the Sung capital in the north, swept south and sacked the towns of Hangchow and Ningpo before being forced back—in A.D. 1131—to a line roughly along the Huai River. Yüeh Fei the Sung commander opposing them was only twenty-nine years old at this time, not only a general commanding the Southern Sung Army but a Chieh Tu Shih, that is a Civil Governor as well. He was confident he could push the Tartar invaders still further back and regain north China, but a policy of appeasement by the then Prime Minister Ch'in Kuei, under the Emperor Kao Tsung, prevailed and led to his recall from the front and imprisonment. He was finally poisoned.

The Emperor Hsiao Tsung, who succeeded Kao Tsung, posthumously reinstated Yüeh Fei. His body was removed from its original burial place outside the Ch'ien-t'ang Gate at Hangchow to the present site, by the shore of the West Lake. A temple was later built, in the following Emperor's reign, adjacent to it, and here one can see today Yüeh Fei's simple tomb with that of his adopted son, Yüeh Yün, beside it.

Guarding the approach to the tomb his generals stand in stone, while, below them and behind two small stone-railed enclosures the iron figures of Ch'in Kuei and his wife, and of two other Ministers responsible for his murder, kneel in penitence.

A man of great courage and an outstanding leader, Yüeh Fei's name has come down through the centuries as representing the highest standard of loyalty to his country.

## 滿江紅　　岳飛

怒髮衝冠憑闌處瀟瀟雨歇抬望眼仰天長嘯壯懷激烈三十功名塵與土八千里路雲和月莫等閒白了少年頭空悲切

靖康恥猶未雪臣子恨何時滅駕長車踏破賀蘭山缺壯志飢餐胡虜肉笑談渴飲匈奴血待從頭收拾舊山河朝天闕

# 56

*P'u – Man Chiang Hung*

Brooding on it, blood boils, bristles prick with rage—
    Hushed now, ceased, the rain-shower's hiss.
    Looking out and up to heaven I roar with rage.
        Passion fires my loyalties.
        Dust, my thirty years of worth and fame;
Miles marched eight thousand; days, nights, parched or chill.
        Who wastes himself and time;
    Still young, lets hair grow white, spirit tame;
        Long will grieve he did so ill.
        Emperor Ching K'ang's shame
        Shouts for vengeance still.
        My hate for palace men
        When shall I fulfil?
    In one fierce chariot charge I'ld break
        The gates of Ho Lan Shan and kill!
My ambition, hungry, is to eat the flesh of Huns;
Later, at my leisure, thirsty, drink the blood I spill!
        Give me my chance again
To win back lake and mountain, stream and plain—
    Then, I'll crave audience of the Emperor!

# LU YU
## (A.D. 1125–1210)

Lu Yu was born a year before Pien-liang (now called K'ai-feng), the capital of the Sungs, was captured by the Nü-chen Tartars. The Chinese Court then retreated south of the Yangtze River and in 1136 the new Emperor set up his capital at Hangchow. Lu Yu entered official service and from Szechuan was keen to go and fight against the invaders. But he was too late to see any active service and retired to his home in Chekiang province.

Some of his poetry (shih) breathes the same spirit, undying if not of quite the same fervour as Yüeh Fei's and Hsin Ch'i Chi's, but a tz'u of a different type has been chosen for this collection. Lu Yu was first married to a girl of the T'ang family with whom he was deeply in love. But his mother did not like her and forced him to divorce her and marry another wife. The divorced girl also re-married. Years later they met, quite by chance, at a friend's tea-party, and this tz'u describes the re-discovery of their undiminished love for one another but likewise the impossibility of gaining their freedom.

One of his last poems was written to his son reminding him to tell his father of the reconquest of China from the Tartars:

I know that everything is empty after death;
  My sole regret, I shall not see the Nine States unified once more.
  But when the Imperial Army, driving north, reoccupies the Central Plain,
  Do not forget to tell your father in your family prayers.

## 釵頭鳳

陸游

紅酥手黃縢酒滿城春色宮牆柳東風惡歡情薄一懷愁緒幾年離索錯錯錯

春如舊人空瘦淚痕紅浥鮫綃透桃花落閒池閣山盟雖在錦書難託莫莫莫

# 57

*P'u – Ch'ai T'ou Feng*

>Crisp pink short-bread,
>A flask of yellow wine,
>The city bright with spring, on palace walls a willow line.
>An east wind, a fierce wind
>Has worn the rapture fine;
>My heart is bound with sorrow round:
>Parted, the many years too long;
>How wrong it was, how wrong!
>
>Spring's the same as ever,
>Vain longings waste and wear;
>My silken handkerchief is soaked, there's blood in every tear.
>Peach blossom scatters round
>The lake and buildings bare.
>Though solemn oath still binds us both
>Its hard to trust a message, so
>It's No! for ever No!

# HSIN CH'I CHI
## (A.D. 1140–1207)

LIKE YÜEH FEI, though not in such a high capacity, Hsin Ch'i Chi fought in his youth against the Nü-chen Tartars; he later entered government service. Also like Yüeh Fei and Lu Yu he took very much to heart the defeat of his country at the hands of these invaders. Much of his poetry, as a result, breathes a manly and heroic spirit for which the tz'u was not, by tradition, a normal vehicle of expression. This led a critic to remark that as Hsin Ch'i Chi had followed his own inclinations—and in doing so had not dealt primarily with the usual themes of separation from friend or lover—then his writings, as tz'u, could not be considered as 'the genuine article'. Fortunately in later years his poetry was increasingly admired. Of the three examples given here one is of the conventional 'separation' type so highly esteemed by the critic.

Hsin Ch'i Chi was fond of including literary allusions in his writings, and evidences of the statesman appear there as well as those of the soldier.

## 醜奴兒

辛棄疾

少年不識愁滋味愛上層樓愛上層樓為賦新詞強說愁

而今識盡愁滋味欲說還休欲說還休卻道天涼好個秋

## 58

*P'u – Ch'ou Nu Erh*

In days when I was young and didn't know the taste of sorrow
        I liked to climb the storied tower,
        I liked to climb the storied tower;
To write the latest odes I forced myself to tell of sorrow.

Now that I understand the taste of sorrow altogether
        I would like to tell, but stop,
        I would like to tell, but stop;
Instead, I say, 'What a cool day! Such lovely autumn weather!'

## 祝英台近　辛棄疾

寶釵分桃葉渡煙柳暗南浦怕上層樓十日九風雨斷腸點點飛紅都無人管更誰勸流鶯聲住　鬢邊覷試把花卜歸期才簪又重數羅帳燈昏哽咽夢中語是他春帶愁來春歸何處卻不解帶將愁去

# 59

*P'u – Chu Ying T'ai Chin*

        Precious hairpin, broken, halved
           At the Peach-Leaf Ferry where
We parted; darkening mist and willow shroud the place.
         I dread to climb the tower-top stair;
Nine days out of ten wind raves, rain torrents race:
It breaks my heart to see the scarlet petals scatter one by one.
          All this with nobody to care
            About it—who is there
         Will bid the oriole's singing cease?

        From mirrored flowers that frame my face
I pluck the petals, try to foretell your return,
      Counting and re-counting them a thousand ways.
          By silken curtains dimly lit
Words born of dreams fight in my throat for release.
It was he, the spring, who brought on me this agony of grief;
          Who knows where spring now strays?
         He did not guess he should have gone
          Taking my grief in his embrace.

## 永遇樂

辛棄疾

千古江山英雄無覓孫仲謀處舞榭歌臺風流總被雨打風吹去斜陽草樹尋常巷陌人道寄奴曾住想當年金戈鐵馬氣吞萬里如虎

元嘉草草封狼居胥贏得倉皇北顧四十三年望中猶記烽火揚州路可堪回首佛貍祠下一片神鴉社鼓憑誰問廉頗老矣尚能飯否

# 60

*P'u - Yung Yü Le*

   Immortal land of peak and river—
   And not a hero to be found
  Though it's Sun Chung Mou's own ground!
   Dancing hall and music chamber,
  These have gone, with rain and wind have gone.
   That grass, those trees at set of sun,
   Those city streets and country lanes:
  Emperor Chi Nu sojourned here, they say.
And I can see him, with his spear of bronze and horse of iron
  Swallowing lands entire as tigers bolt their prey!

   In Emperor Yüan Chia's muddled reign
  He thought to add lustre to the Lang Chü Hsü—
   A hasty glance up North his single feat!
    Forty three years ago!
   Looking across I still remember
    The Yangchow beacons blazing opposite.
   But how can I endure to think
  Of other days by Fo Li's shrine,
Hearing the temple crows and drums of celebration beat?
   Who comes to ask me now
   'Does General Lien Po seem too old?'
  'Does he still eat as once he used to eat?'

## 摸魚兒

辛棄疾

更能消幾番風雨怨怱怱春又歸去惜春長怕花開早何況落紅無數春且住見說道天涯芳草無歸路怨春不語算祗有殷勤畫簷蛛網盡日惹飛絮　長門事準擬佳期又誤蛾眉曾有人妒千金縱買相如賦脈脈此情誰訴君莫舞君不見玉環飛燕皆塵土閑愁最苦休去倚危闌斜陽正在煙柳斷腸處

# 61

*P'u – Mo Yü Erh*

    How many tempests still in store can spring withstand?
      So soon, too soon, and it will vanish out of hand.
  Lovers of spring must always care when flowers bloom too early;
Then how much more to see their countless petals strew the land.
          Spring, for a while, then, stay!
I've heard it said the grasses spread so thick to the horizon, none returns that way.
        Spring, vexing spring, respond, I say!
        I must admit at least you're diligent:
    Trapped in the spider's webs under the eaves
    The willow-down you drove to flight all day!

          That tale of tight shut doors!
  Of course they'll still contrive to deny me an audience.
    Beauty was the reason once why others' envy grew.
But even if I squandered gold on pleas by Hsiang Ju
    Who's likely to pay heed to feelings so intense?
         Sirs, dancing will not do!
Have you forgotten then that Kuei Fei and Fei Yen are nothing now but dust?
    The lonely learn grief through and through.
I should not lean like this on the high railing,
    For it is there the sun is dying,
  Where misty willows tear the heart in two.

# CHIANG K'UEI
(A.D. 1150–1230)

CHIANG K'UEI was both a poet and composer of music; some of his music for tz'u have come down to us. Of delicate build, very hospitable though poor, and a collector of books and scrolls, he seems to have been a man of great charm.

Fan Ch'eng Ta, a great military governor, historian and naturalist, some twenty-five years his senior, was so struck by Chiang K'uei's compositions of music and lyrics in a new style that he presented him with one of his own household girls, Hsiao Hung. This girl was almost certainly the inspiration of the poem (No. 62) included in this collection. It was written when he was 37 years old and on the following New Year's Eve he took her home with him.

暗香　石湖詠梅　姜夔

舊時月色算幾番照我梅邊吹笛喚起玉人不管清寒與攀摘何遜而今漸老都忘卻春風詞筆但怪得竹外疏花香冷入瑤席　江國正寂寂歎寄與路遙夜雪初積翠尊易泣紅萼無言耿相憶長記曾攜手處千樹壓西湖寒碧又片片吹盡也幾時見得

# 62

*P'u – An Hsiang*

      Moonlight of days long overcome,
    How many times it shone on me as I,
       Piping my flute beside the plum,
    Aroused your beauty with a serenade.
What cared I for the cold, or if you picked the spring blossom?
  I sang then like Ho Hsün!—but now that I grow old
The lyric note is quite forgot, the voice of spring is dumb.
Yet still I marvel as from scattered flowers beyond the canes
    Cool scented airs into my bedroom come.

         On field and river
        An utter stillness lies.
  So long the road; and now the night-snows mass
    All I can send as presents are my sighs.
     This bowl of jade moves me to tears;
Mutely, this blossom conjures up shared shining memories.
   But always I recall that walk when hand in hand
We saw the ice-green Western Lake clasped by a thousand trees.
     Now every leaf is blown away.
   When shall we see again what memory sees?

## 揚州慢　　姜夔

淮左名都，竹西佳處，解鞍少駐初程。過春風十里，盡薺麥青青。自胡馬窺江去後，廢池喬木猶厭言兵。漸黃昏清角吹寒，都在空城。

杜郎俊賞，算而今重到須驚。縱豆蔻詞工，青樓夢好，難賦深情。二十四橋仍在，波心蕩冷月無聲。念橋邊紅藥，年年知為誰生。

# 63

*P'u - Yang Chou Man*

>Far-famed city east of the River Huai;
>>Haven of beauty west of the bamboos!
>Stop, we'll loosen the saddles and rest now we have seen
>The first stage through, ten miles in the wind of spring;
>>Wild flowers everywhere, wheat the greenest of green.
>So it has been since the Tartar horse turned back at the river:
>>Even the ruined lakes and trees
>>Are loth to say what happened then.
>>As twilight slowly falls
>>A soldier's horn, clear on the cold wind,
>>Is all this empty city knows of men.

>>Tu Mu once elegantly praised it;
>>Now, it's not hard to guess
>>His shock, could he come back again!
>>Even with his poetic skill
>>And dreams about his Azure Tower
>>His feelings would be too deep to express.
>All the twenty-four bridges are still left standing,
>>But only waves go past
>>And the cold and silent moon.
>Look where the flowers grow down by the bridge there;
>For whom do they blossom now, I wonder, as the years flow on?

## 疏影 　　　　姜夔

苔枝綴玉，有翠禽小小，枝上同宿。客裏相逢，籬角黃昏，無言自倚修竹。昭君不慣胡沙遠，但暗憶江南江北。想佩環月夜歸來，化作此花幽獨。

猶記深宮舊事，那人正睡裏，飛近蛾綠。莫似春風，不管盈盈，早與安排金屋。還教一片隨波去，又卻怨玉龍哀曲。等恁時重覓幽香，已入小窗橫幅。

# 64

Ode to the Plum Blossom

*P'u – Su Ying*

        Mossy branches, jade-white blossom,
      Tiniest of tiny birds in malachite green
      Perched on the branches resting together:
        Guests all of us, meeting each other
        Beside the fence in a twilit corner;
  Hushed against the bamboo hedge the plum trees lean.

Chao Chün, so unused to the Tartars' life far-off in the alien
    desert,
Only in secret remembered her own land north and south of the
    river.
  I think she came one moonlit night wearing her tinkling girdle
  And took the shape of these unfriended flowers for ever.

    I still recall the old tale: in the depths of the palace,
      Just as sleep had come to enfold the princess,
      On to her forehead a plum-blossom fell.
      Nothing can match the spring-wind's callous
        Way with blossoming loveliness—
Early, come early enough to prepare them a golden room!

For now the last of all the petals is borne away on the waters
And I cannot abide that song of the Jade Dragon flute so laden
    with woe;
  And think, if you want to rediscover that exquisite scent, its
    bloom
  Will only be found on the scroll over the small window.

# LIU K'O CHUANG
## (A.D. 1187–1269)

A NATIVE of Fukien Province, he came of a well-established family and served in a variety of Government posts. He earned a considerable reputation in his life-time as a poet, using the tz'u to express his thoughts clearly and without the use of elliptical language.

The short example of his work included in this collection illustrates the clarity, economy, and the depth of thought underlying the apparent simplicity of his approach.

## 卜算子　　　劉克莊

片片蝶衣輕,點點猩紅小,道是天公不惜花,百種千般巧。　朝見樹頭繁,暮見枝頭少,道是天公果惜花,雨洗風吹了。

# 65

*P'u – Pu Suan Tzu*

Leaf by leaf as light as a butterfly's wing,
Speck by speck of scarlet in dots so small;
Some people say that God lacks any concern for leaf or flower.
The myriad-formed! The skill that fashioned them all!

See the tree-tops laden with leaf at morning,
See the branches stripped by the end of day.
Some people say that God undoubtedly cares for leaf and flower.
The rain has swept them, the wind has blown them away!

# WU WEN YING
(A.D. 1200–1260 approx.)

A POET with great delicacy of expression, who much appealed to the man in the street. This poem, like many others of his, was undoubtedly written about his runaway concubine Ch'ü Chi. As of Wen T'ing Yün the criticism was levelled at Wu Wen Ying that separate lines of his tz'u shone with a brilliance that the poems lacked as a whole.

## 風入松　　吳文英

聽風聽雨過清明愁草瘞花銘樓前綠暗分攜路一絲柳一寸柔情料峭春寒中酒迷離曉夢啼鶯　西園日日掃林亭依舊賞新晴黃蜂頻撲秋千索有當時纖手香凝惆悵雙鴛不到幽階一夜苔生

# 66

*P'u – Feng Ju Sung*

I hear the wind, I hear the rain as the Ch'ing Ming passes by.
Heaped under meagre grass dead blossoms lie.
Facing the house, deep leaf shadows the road where we said farewell:
A willow tendril waves
Each quivering inch responsively.
Lately, in spring's cold mood, when wine had warmed my rest,
Half roused at dreaming dawn I heard the oriole cry.

Daily I sweep the cabin in the western garden trees.
The sun shines as of old and the golden bees
Fly unceasingly to and fro haunting the ropes on the swing
Which harbour from those days
Scent of soft hands, and memories.
That pair of Mandarin ducks, how sad they never came.
Moss on deserted steps has spread by night its fleece.

## CHIANG CHIEH

(*circa* 1270)

A NATIVE of Kiangsu Province he passed his doctorate in A.D. 1275 under the Southern Sungs and then retired to Chu Shan when the Mongols (Yüan Dynasty) conquered the south. Though recommended for Government employment in A.D. 1297 he refused to take office under the new dynasty.

In this tz'u he pictures himself on his travels 'up-country' as a Government official, longing for home and spring at home.

## 一剪梅

蒋捷

一片春愁待酒浇江上舟摇楼上帘招秋娘渡与泰娘桥风又飘飘雨又萧萧　何日归家洗客袍银字笙调心字香烧流光容易把人抛红了樱桃绿了芭蕉

# 67

*P'u – I Chien Mei*

Such grief for spring possesses me it cries aloud for wine.
On the river boats are rocking,
From the shop an inn-sign beckons.
Down at the ford of Ch'iu Niang, at the bridge of T'ai Niang
Swirling gusts go whirling, twirling
Past the rain-shower's whistling hiss.

When shall I reach home again and wash my travelling clothes,
Play upon the silver flute,
Light the heart-shaped frankincense?
Time flows on and quickly passes, leaving us behind:
Cherries, look, are flushed already,
Plantains boast a new-born green.

# YÜAN DYNASTY

## SA TU LA

(A.D. 1308–?)

SA TU LA was a Mongol. He was almost certainly born in China and lived in Yen-Men in Shansi Province. (The Mongols of Genghiz Khan's Army had moved south in A.D. 1211 to attack the Nü-chen Tartars who were installed at that time in North China as the Chin Dynasty. Genghiz Khan then turned his attention to the west, but his descendants later came back to the attack on China, and resuming their advance southwards captured Hangchow, the capital of the Southern Sungs, in 1276.)

He passed the Civil Service doctorate examination of chin-shih and eventually rose to the important post of Governor of Fukien Province.

Himself a descendant of foreign invaders he would not have the same feelings as those which moved Yüeh Fei and Hsin Ch'i Chi to plead for the recovery of China's lost territory taken by the Nü-chen Tartars, or Chiang K'uei to lament over the city of Yangchow devastated by them. Sa Tu La's lament was not over a plundered city but over the fallen fortunes of Chin-ling (Nanking), once the capital and a thriving and gay city at the time of the Six Dynasties (A.D. 420–589). It was the reaction of a man caught up in the hurly-burly and continuous wining and feasting inseparable from the life of an important official, when confronted with this sad example of the transitoriness of human glories.

念奴嬌　　　　薩都拉

石頭城上望天低吳楚眼中無物指點六朝形勝地惟有青山如壁薇日旌旗連雲檣艫白骨紛如雪一江南北消磨多少豪傑

寂寞避暑離宮東風輦路芳草年年發落日無人松逕冷鬼火高低明滅歌舞尊前繁華鏡裏暗換青青髮傷心千古春誰一片明月

# 68

*P'u – Nien Nu Chiao*

Look high, look low
Over the stone-walled city;
Of the Kingdoms of Wu and Ch'u nothing is left to see.
Point to the places known to fame
Throughout the Six Dynasties;
Green hills like a wall are the only memory.
Banners once obscured the sunlight,
Masts of vessels met the clouds:
Now whitened bones are spread like snow.
North and south of the Great River,
How many heroes perished so?

They came to the secluded summer palace to escape the heat;
But now the east wind sweeps the royal road
And grass grows rankly year by year.
In the setting sun it's cold under
The pines; no-one's about:
Will-o'-the-wisps play high, play low, shine brightly, disappear.
What nights of song, of dance and feasting!
Hair in the mirror shows
A stealthy change from dark to grey.
In hearts of men an endless sorrow flows;
Radiant under the moon stretches the Ch'in Huai.

## 滿江紅　　　　薩都拉

六代豪華，春去也，更無消息。空悵望，山川形勝，已非疇昔。王謝堂前雙燕子，烏衣巷口曾相識。聽夜深寂寞打孤城，春潮急。

思往事，愁如織。懷故國，空陳跡。但荒煙衰草，亂鴉斜日。玉樹歌殘秋露冷，胭脂井壞寒螿泣。到如今只有蔣山青，秦淮碧。

# 69

*P'u – Man Chiang Hung*

>The gay glory of the Six Dynasties
>   Has vanished like the spring,
>      Its message lost for evermore.
>         You guess in vain
>   What all these hills and rivers meant to men before;
>      There's been such change in everything.
>And yet—a pair of swallows used to haunt the halls of Wang
>         and Hsieh;
>   Surely I saw them fly just now into the mouth of Blackcoat
>         Lane!
>         Late in the night I hear
>   No sound except the spring tide lap the abandoned city
>         And then speed on again.

>         Thoughts of the long ago
>         Are interwoven with grief.
>         The realms of legend fade
>            To traces bald and brief:
>         Only a wisp of mist and withered grasses
>      And crows off home as daylight passes.
>   The Jade Tree song's no longer heard in the cold autumn
>         dew;
>      Down in the ruined Well of Shame only the crickets
>         mourn.
>         Yet up to now
>         Mount Chiang has kept its green
>            Ch'in Huai its blue.

# MING
DYNASTY

## LIU CHI (Po Wen)
### (A.D. 1311–1375)

LIU CHI was born in the time of the Yüan (Mongol) Dynasty but the last seven years of his life were spent under the Mings. It was in return for his help to the Mings in their gaining control of the country that he was given an important ministerial job (T'ai Shih Ling) at the capital. A scholar and statesman, he had the reputation of being hard and unbending.

The conventional note of separation in the single tz'u included—the woman longing for her absent lover—is saved from banality by its keen observation and economy.

## 眼兒媚　　　劉基

萋萋煙草小樓西，雲壓雁聲低，兩行疏柳，一絲殘照，萬點鴉棲。　春山碧樹秋重綠，人在武陵溪，無情明月，有情歸夢，同到幽閨。

## 70

*P'u – Yen Erh Mei*

West of the little tower the smoky grass has grown a fleece;
    Blanketing cloud muffles the cry of the geese;
        A slender pair of willow rows,
        A single thread of fading light,
    A thousand specks, the roosting crows.

The mountain trees like jade in spring, how green their autumn look;
    Her man's away beside the Wu Ling brook.
        The loveless light of the bright moon,
        The love-filled dream of his return
    Together flood her lonely room.

# CH'ING DYNASTY

# NA-LAN HSING-TE
(A.D. 1655–1685)

NA-LAN HSING-TE was a Manchu. He was a Guards officer at the Palace and appears to have fallen in love with one of the Imperial concubines with whom marriage was of course impossible.

The Ch'ing (Manchu) dynasty had already been on the throne of China eleven years before he was born. Thus he grew up thinking of Peking as 'home' and refers to it as such even when describing with such point and brevity a visit to the country of his nomadic ancestors in Manchuria (see p. 207).

长相思

纳兰性德

山一程水一程身向榆关那畔行夜深千帐灯

风一更雪一更聒碎乡心梦不成故园无此声

# 71

*P'u – Ch'ang Hsiang Ssu*

        The mountain, a march;
        The river, a march;
To the uplands and over the Yü Kuan Pass I go.
  Countless lamps in the tented darkness glow.

        A night-watch of wind,
        A night-watch of snow—
And a clamour that shatters my sleepless home-sick heart.
    I know a garden where it is not so.

画堂春　　纳兰性德

一生一代一双人，争教两处销魂相
思相望不相亲，天为谁春

浆向蓝
桥易乞，药成碧海难奔　若容相访饮
牛津相对忘贫

# 72

*P'u – Hua T'ang Ch'un*

One gift of years; one pulse of time; one pair of souls, we two.
    Why do we let love overwhelm us, life divide us?
Eyes meet, thoughts meet, but we, we never meet as lovers do.
    Heaven made the spring for someone; who?

    Easier far to beg for liquid jade at the Blue
Bridge; and hard to pierce heaven's seas though magic tide us.
If we drank water from the cattle-ford, though poor, yet you
    And I would meet as lovers do!

# TSO FU

(A.D. 1751–1833)

Tso Fu was a Kiangsu man by birth. He passed his doctorate into government service, became a magistrate at Anhwei and later Governor of Hunan Province. He established a reputation in his day for writing poetry, both shih and tz'u.

Tso Fu, in the poem here, makes an expedition to Hsün-yang in the hopes of being able to see or hear the spirits of the girl with the guitar and the traveller—two characters in Po Chü I's famous poem 'P'i P'a Hsing' (the Song of the Guitar) written about 1000 years earlier (see Appendix II, Poem 73, p. 244).

南浦夜尋琵琶亭　　左輔

潯陽江上恰三更霜月共潮生斷岸高低向我漁火一星ミ何處雜聲刮起
撥琵琶千載騰空亭是江湖倦客飄零商婦于此盪精靈　且自
移船相近遶迴關百折覓愁魂我是無家張儉萬里走江城一例蒼茫弔
古向荻花楓葉又傷心只琵琶響斷魚龍寂寞不曾醒

# 73

*P'u – Nan P'u*

        On the Hsün-yang River
Frost fell at the third watch, as moon and tide rose together.
     Facing me, the bank curved in dips and ridges;
       Lights from fishermen shone, each a star.
Where was that song of parting sung, the sound of a guitar
Thrumming a thousand years ago? The empty shelter still is
             there.
        He, the way-worn passer-by;
      The merchant's wife, a driven leaf.
   Here, it must be here their spirits wander!

        And I brought my boat in closer,
Walking round the curved gunwale seeking those sad souls.
      Homeless, a wanderer like Chang Chien,
      Travelling countless miles by city and river,
  At ease in desolate haunts of men, I search in the past.
And finding here the plumed rushes and maple leaves my heart
           was touched.
       Only, I heard no sound of a guitar.
       Fish and dragon slept, deep and still.

# NOTE ON THE TZ'U

## Its Development and Ornamentation

THE TZ'U has been composed now for some 1200 years, having been clearly identified as a style of poetry in its own right during the T'ang Dynasty (A.D. 600–900). But to see how it developed, one must look first at the traditional forms of Chinese poetry.

From the earliest forms, the ballad type, of the Shih Ching (written before 500 B.C.) there was gradually built up a type of verse, called 'shih', which became progressively stylized by the time of the T'angs. Regularity of length of line (usually either of five or seven characters to a line) in any one poem, regularity of rhyme (the second line of each couplet rhyming with the second line of the next) and a moderate use of parallelism laid down the pattern. With the civil service examination system including the Classics and the writing of this traditional verse as one of its most important parts, and with faultlessness of style and precision of form as the main criteria in these examinations, it is hardly surprising that the pattern of the country's poetry was gradually put into a strait jacket and poets began reaching out into other, less formal, patterns. It was in the T'ang Dynasty that possibly the most significant turn in this direction was given, and of the many theories put forward to explain the development of the tz'u the introduction of foreign music seems to be one of the important factors. As a result of the freer flow of people from foreign countries visiting this flourishing Empire, a great deal of foreign music was introduced. The tunes caught on but they needed Chinese words. Some of these lyrics were supplied by existing poems of the traditional pattern—the shih—which, if they did not fit the tune exactly, were filled out with meaningless sounds, like the fol-de-rols in certain English lyrics. But gradually there came a vogue for writing lyrics specifically for the tunes.

The first poem in this collection, by the great writer of traditional poetry Li Po, looks at first sight to be an ordinary 'shih' with a verse of four lines, each line of seven characters. But we know that this poem was indeed set to music if not written for music—to be played on the flute—and it is classed as 'tz'u', a lyric.

The second poem (p. 7), by the same author, goes a stage further in adopting the typical irregularity in length of line which is associated with the tz'u, to fit a tune. From this time on we are dealing with the situation that either the tune itself set the pattern, or when the tune had been forgotten, the form it had taken remained as a pattern into which the lyric had to be fitted.

Developed in this way during the flowering of Chinese literature under the T'ang Dynasty, the tz'u reached its own highest development under the Sungs (in the period between A.D. 1000–1200), and is written to this day. Although it is generally held that there was a period of decline from the end of the Sung Dynasty until there came a revival in the Ch'ing Dynasty, there is still a consecutive period of about 500 years under the T'ang and Sung Emperors when the tz'u came to be as highly valued as the shih.

The classical examination system was the first step towards a highly centralised civil service. This bred, as a result of son following in a father's footsteps, a clique of literati educated far above the level of the rest of the population. To be able to give expression to their talents they would meet especially to exchange poems, compose, cap each other's efforts and build up parallel pairs of lines. These literary parties were by no means confined to men only and did not as a rule take place in a man's home.

A man's marriage would have been arranged for him, probably while he was still a child; his bride was usually taken on unseen before the wedding day, and was unlikely to have been educated to read and write poetry. She was regarded as a housekeeper, possibly as an expert in needlework and embroidery, as a vehicle for procreation, but usually not as an intellectual companion. Intellectual companionship the educated man often sought from company outside his home, either with his fellow literati or with the courtesans and singing girls. These latter were quite often educated in so far as they could at least talk the language of poetry that their clientele brought to the establishment. Poems were of course written to wives, daughters, sons, brothers and fellow scholars, but the very nature of the tz'u and its association with music tended to suit it to a wide public in this free life of outside entertainment. Much, therefore, of the great body of 'love poetry' (some of it very moving) refers to life in this milieu, and the highest in the land did not exclude themselves from it.

One poet, Chou Pang Yen, was visiting a famous courtesan Li Shih Shih one evening when the Emperor, also one of the girl's admirers, was announced. Chou Pang Yen dived under the bed and the next day wrote the following verse (reprinted here for convenience) based on observations from his hiding place; at that period the orange was a rarity.

> Knife from Ping as bright as water,
> Salt from Wu surpassing snow,
> An orange rare her slender fingers tear.
> Newly warmed embroidered curtains,
> Incense from the dragon burner;
> Playing the sheng they face each other there.
>
> Her low voice softly asks
> 'Where are you going to spend the night?
> They've called the third watch from the city wall.
> Your horse will slip, the frost's so thick;
> You'd do much better not to go;
> There's hardly anyone about at all.'

The poem, of course, got back to the Emperor's ears and Chou was dismissed from his post. When Li Shih Shih saw him off from the capital he wrote her some farewell lines which she later read out to the Emperor. He was so moved by them that he reinstated Chou as Director of the Musical Academy.

Many of the great lyric writers were civil servants brought up in centres of culture among friends of similar tastes, and forced in the course of their career to travel over an enormous empire on administrative and sometimes military duties. As a result families were often separated and lesser connections broken. The contrast between life in the capital and conditions 'up-country' was harsh. Seasonal contrast in a continental climate was equally harsh. A man might be away for a year or more on a tour of inspection, or he might be stationed in some outpost of the empire expecting nothing more than transfer to another remote corner, and the less successful (or more out of favour) he was the further away from the capital his posting. He would long for the companionship of his own kind, for love and for metropolitan delights. Spring, most treasured of the seasons, came and went in a flash; the spring flowers were withered by the sun and the petals scattered by parching winds. Hence the recurring themes of loss and separation, of intolerable nostalgia seeking an outlet in poetry. Only occasionally, as in Yen Shu's poem (No. 33), do we read about unshadowed joy. And only once in this collection, in Liu K'o Chuang's poem (No. 65) is there any reference to a divine interest in creation, questionably benevolent.

Such enforced separation encouraged the creative faculties in lonely men burning to share the expression of their thoughts and feelings with others. Strong friendships between one scholar and another would be continued in correspondence and once again the exchange of verse and of criticism would continue hundreds of miles apart.

Many phrases, repeated again and again, reflect the grief of separation. For instance the storied building, or tower, which would probably be a single one in the group of single-storied halls and sleeping apartments clustered round a series of courtyards, would be resorted to by the solitary watcher. There is an attractive poem by Hsin Ch'i Chi (reprinted here for convenience) referring to this.

> When I was young and didn't know the taste of sorrow
> > I liked to climb the storied tower,
> > I liked to climb the storied tower;
> To write the latest odes I forced myself to tell of sorrow.
>
> Now that I understand the taste of sorrow altogether
> > I would like to tell, but stop,
> > I would like to tell, but stop;
> Instead, I say 'What a cool day! Such lovely autumn weather!'

It would be from these towers, or in buildings of more than the usual single storey, that a woman would look out towards the horizon beyond which her husband or loved one would be stationed. There she would 'lean on the railing' brooding on her thoughts, having gone to elaborate trouble over her hairstyle—note the 'Plum' style hair display mentioned in Poem 37—and make-up. Great attention was paid to a woman's hair, and rouge and powder were in common use, as was also pencilling of the eyebrows. A Han Dynasty official was reported to the Emperor for improper behaviour because he was seen, in his own house, painting his wife's eyebrows. He submitted in defence that surely in the privacy of his own home such behaviour could not be censured. The Emperor dismissed the case against him.

Transfer from one post to another led to the frequent references to travel. The means of travel would be more often than not by canal or river, from jetties usually just outside the city gates (see Poems 41 and 51). With its western boundaries flanked by the great Central Asian mountain ranges, China's great rivers, the Yangtze and the Yellow River as well as many others, flow eastwards. This is often quoted in Chinese poetry as a natural phenomenon as if applicable to all rivers (see Li Yü's Poems 18 and 25). Whether travel was by land or water there would be resting places and shelters, the bigger ones set up at intervals of ten Chinese miles (about $3\frac{1}{2}$ English miles) and smaller ones at intermediate half-way intervals (see the last line of Poem 3).

Once having arrived at his station the official would have plenty of time for his literary recreation, and for the observation of birds and cultivation of flowers. It is interesting to see the poet Yen Shu writing of the almost positive recognition of bird migration involving the return from their winter quarters of individual swallows, whereas in the Western world, until a very much later date, our forbears talked of swallows hibernating in the mud of ponds as an explanation for their disappearance in autumn and reappearance in the same place in spring. Fan Chung Yen (see Poem 28) speaks of the autumn southward migration of geese as commonplace knowledge.

This is not to say that these poets did not enjoy and make use of a full share of legend and superstition, such as stories of the mythical phoenix which would only rest in one sort of tree—the wu t'ung tree (see Li Yü's Poem 19 and Appendix II, p. 234). It was in fact the tendency in the poets who followed after the Sung Dynasty to resort more and more to classical allusions, literary, historical and mythological, which not only make their poetry too abstruse even for the average Chinese but leave it almost impossible to put into readable English verse (see for instance Na-lan Hsing-te, Poem 72).

Li Yü's mention (see Poem 22) of the geese having flown in, 'yet there's no trace of news', may well have been simply a statement of fact, but there is a well-known literary allusion to a legend of the second century B.C. The Emperor Wu Ti of the Han Dynasty at that time sent one of his officials Su Wu to negotiate with the Hsiung Nu 'Barbarians' in the north-west. The legend has it that in the course of an enforced stay of several decades in the Mongolian desert he managed to fix a message to the leg of a wild goose before its southward migration. The goose was shot by the Han Emperor, who was thus able to take steps to secure Su Wu's release. As we now know, it is by no means an impossible feat to secure a goose in the moulting season after breeding, when they are unable to fly, and the legend of Su Wu may not be as far-fetched as would appear at first sight.

Few of the old tunes survive, and though some of those used by Chiang K'uei (see p. 169) have come down to us, there is no example of any lyrics based on their tune-pattern in this particular collection. One melody probably composed in the Yüan (Mongol) Dynasty has been attached to the same tune-pattern used by the poet Ch'in Kuan under the tune-title 'I Wang Sun' (see p. 133). The tune on page 220 occurs in T'ung Fei's Chung Yüeh Hsün Yüan (ch. shang, f. 87, r). While this tune was probably written about three hundred years later than Ch'in Kuan's poem and while the style of the music would undoubtedly have changed and become more enriched since the earlier date, nevertheless we may get some inkling of the sort of haunting melody that Ch'in Kuan would have had in mind.

Each tz'u in a Chinese anthology is preceded by the name of the tune (p'u) which prescribed the pattern of the verse, but which seldom has any connection with its subject. No attempt in general has been made in this collection either to make up titles for the poems, or to translate the Chinese titles for the tune-patterns; an exception has been made in one or two instances when the poet has himself a prefatory note about the subject of the poem (e.g. Su Shih prefaces Poem No. 46 by the

note 'Cherished thoughts on the Red Cliff' which has been rendered here simply as 'Ode to the Red Cliff') and in one instance (Su Shih's Poem No. 47) where reference to the subject matter seemed to be helpful in the English. The names of the tune-patterns (or tune-titles) are available to readers of the Chinese versions and are also noted at the head of each poem under the poem number in the transliterated form (Wade) of Chinese. An English translation is almost always without significance (for instance Hsin Ch'i Chi's poem No. 58 is to a tune called 'The Ugly Slave Girl'), and when differently interpreted by two translators—as often occurs—can be misleading rather than helpful.

Enjoying such full cadenced translations as we have had in the great work of Arthur Waley and of those few translators of the stature of Witter Bynner, a reader, ignorant of Chinese, may be excused if he imagines that the Chinese poet always wrote with the same fluid mastery as the translator, subject to no strict rules of rhyme, rhythm and form, let alone, in the case of the lyric, of tonal pattern. But if the aim is to reflect as far as possible the pattern of Chinese poetry in English rather than to produce English poetry from the Chinese, an added reason for a return to the attitude taken up by the earlier translators and versifiers—like for instance the scholar H. A. Giles—is that the Chinese themselves plainly miss in today's translations of their favourite lyrics some of the ornamentation that appeals so much in their own language. Apart from the obvious one of calligraphy, already mentioned in the Preface, the forms of ornamentation might be listed as rhyme, pattern and rhythm, parallel-ism or 'pairing', alliterations and onomatopoeia, and last but not least, though of course it cannot be reflected in any other language, the tonal pattern or melodic rhythm of the lyric. To deal with these then in turn.

*(a) Rhyme*

The Chinese language is unusually rich in rhyme, and all Chinese poetry (up to the twentieth century) is rhymed and each couplet, and very often each line, is end-stopped. In the tz'u it is not unknown for every line to end on the same rhyme and common for more than half the lines in a poem to rhyme. This obviously makes for great difficulty in our language which is notably poor in rhyming sounds. One famous English author has expressed the view that 'a rhymed translation can only be a paraphrase and is apt to fall back on padding'. Another, again of translations from the Chinese, has written that he hopes that 'there will be an end to all attempts at rhyme'. But how is it possible, with such formal verse, to convey the poet's intention without exploring in translation his architectural design? To the Chinese reader, the discipline and ornamentations of these poems are essential to their enjoyment. The poet, writing to a prescribed pattern, must have planned his total effect with all the banked-up fire that once made the rondeau and the sonnet burn so brightly in the service of inspired talent.

Too much cannot be expected. Apart from difficulties already mentioned, the absence in general from Chinese poetry of verbal inflection, genders and pronouns, prepositions and conjunctions, and its epigrammatic and allusive qualities, provide their own humbling difficulties, both in translation and in subsequent versification. Nevertheless, if the will is there to follow the rhyme-patterns and tune-patterns up to, but only up to, the limits beyond which the versifier turns into a clumsy verbal acrobat, and provided the result is an acceptable translation, it is worth while making the attempt.

The rhyming in this collection sometimes faithfully follows the Chinese pattern all the way. Rhyme is generally preserved as an ornament, but is sometimes abandoned where it is plainly going to spoil the effectiveness of the English verse. In one case, in the poem by Chang Chieh (see Poem 67) where the rhyme in Chinese is not only the same on all twelve lines but is augmented internally by onomatopœia—using the same rhyme—effort was concentrated on trying to convey the Chinese rollicking urgent rhythm, and rhyme was not introduced at all. Transliteration of the Chinese reads as follows, the rhyming sounds —ending in the English 'ao', as in 'how'—being underlined:

    I p'ien ch'un ch'ou tai chiu chi*ao*
        Chiang shang chou y*ao*
        Lou shang lien ch*ao*
    Ch'iu Niang Tu yü T'ai Niang Ch'i*ao*
        Feng yu p'*iao* p'*iao*
        Yü yu hsi*ao* hsi*ao*

        Ho jih kuei chia hsi k'o p'*ao*
        Yin tzu sheng ti*ao*
        Hsin tzu hsiang sh*ao*
    Liu kuang jung i pa jen p'*ao*
        Hung liao ying t'*ao*
        Lü liao pa chi*ao*

If possible the reader should try to hear this poem in the original—a Chinese Restaurant Manager shown the Chinese version will probably be delighted to recite it, and in fact will possibly know it.

## (b) Pattern and Rhythm

Though the traditional way of writing and printing tz'u, as was mentioned in the Preface, masks the irregularity in the length of the lines, Wen T'ing Yün's Poem (No. 6) is written

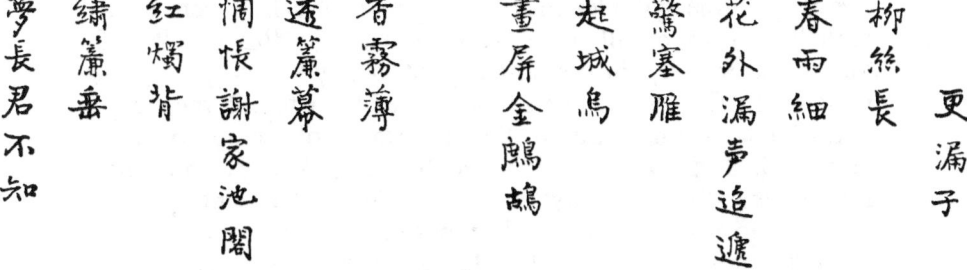

Tune—pattern 'Keng Lou Tzu'
Tz'u (poem No. 6) by Wen T'ing Yün
written out to show irregularity in length of lines.

out above, starting from the top right corner and reading vertically down line by line, to show the tune-pattern (Keng Lou Tzu) for this particular poem. (The six characters on the extreme right give first the tune-title and then the poet's name below.) Reference to Appendix III will show that this pattern is in fact 3-3-6-3-3-5; 3-3-6-3-3-5.

In each line, each character (not absolutely invariably but generally) had to conform in tone to the pattern set for the particular tune; composition of a lyric was therefore a work of art in fitting in words to suit, precisely, a prescribed pattern. This fitting in is the facet of the tz'u which makes it much more difficult to compose than the traditional style of poem—the shih. It must be explained first that in classical Chinese (now and during the period covered in this collection, if not earlier) each character carries its own tone. This tone may be one of four —a high level, a rising, a falling and an 'entering' (or clipped) tone. A sequence of these tones gives a melodic flowing rhythm, and there were certain basic guides to be observed if a line was to read euphoniously; for instance it would not sound attractive if all three syllables in the end group of a line were on a high level tone or all on a falling tone. It is this quality of 'organized melody' in the language of poetry which gives prominence in Chinese to the sound rather than to the meaning, and which leads naturally to the importance of reciting poetry, and particularly tz'u, aloud. After the Sung Dynasty and until recent times the tonal rhythm of the tz'u has been interpreted as being governed by two main types of tones 'p'ing' and 'tse', the level and deflected tones. But scholarship is revealing an even more complicated pattern of melody which was followed by the poet. For instance the 'p'ing-tse' analysis fails to illustrate fully the tz'u of the poet Chou Pang Yen where all four tones can be seen to be used in an established sequence in the tune-pattern Lang T'ao Sha Man.

Quite apart from this melodic rhythm, it must be remembered that the characters in a line are seldom read without a pause. In a typical tz'u (say Li Yü's Poem No. 19), each line would be read out loud with short pauses, shown below by a stroke, as follows (there being a longer pause at the end of the line):

        Wu yen / tu shang / hsi lou
            Yüeh / ju kou
Chi mo / wu t'ung / shen yüan / so ch'ing ch'iu
          Chien / pu tuan
           Li / hai luan
          Shih li ch'ou
Pieh shih / i pan / tzu wei / tsai hsin t'ou.

Note: for refinements in this pattern of pauses the reader is referred to Dr. K. P. K. Whitaker's article 'Some Notes on the Tsyr' printed in the Bulletin of the School of Oriental and African Studies (University of London), Vol. XIV, Part 1.


(c) *Parallel-ism*

Parallel-ism or the 'pairing' of lines in a poem is another of the forms of ornamentation with a particular appeal to Chinese eyes. Two lines, of the same number of characters, to be paired had to correspond not only in synonymous or antithetical meaning; but each character with its opposing character in the next line, verb with verb; and noun with noun; indeed if the pair was to be regarded as perfect, correspondence had to go to the extent of paralleling the type of noun or verb in consecutive lines—as 'flowers' with 'trees', or 'advance' with 'retreat'.

There is a story told that the great poet Su Shih's sister, who was, exceptionally, a talented poetess in her own right, shut the door on her newly-wed husband on their first night with the remark that she would not open it until he had successfully paired a line of seven characters which read:

Shut — doors* — push out — window — in front — moon
(*i.e. two halves of the window)

that is to say colloquially 'Shutting the window has pushed the moonlight outside'. The unfortunate bridegroom paced up and down quite unable to complete the other half, when Su Shih himself arrived on the scene. Unwilling to spoil the game too obviously, he threw a pebble on to the glassy surface of the pond outside the door as he passed, whereupon the young man was at once able to write down:

Throw—stone—break open—water—at the bottom of—sky
(that is 'Throwing a stone has broken open the sky at the bottom of the pond').

The tz'u's irregular length of line obviously did not lend itself so readily to pairing, but such was the hold of this type of ornamentation, that there are instances when pairing of two consecutive lines of equal length is prescribed in certain tz'u patterns. (For example of this see the fifth and sixth lines of Ou Yang Hsiu's Poem No. 38.)

## (d) Alliteration and Onomatopoeia

As may be imagined with the accent thrown so heavily on the sound of the poem when recited, the Chinese made full use of alliteration, onomatopoeia, and rhyming compounds in a line.

Huang T'ing Chien, for instance, makes particular use of rhyme and alliteration in his Poem No. 49. All lines, except the fifth, end on the same rhyme. Then the first two characters of the poem 'Tung feng' are a rhyming pair (or compound), as are the last two characters of the fifth line 'Lung feng'. There is alliteration in the third line 'ling lo' and at the end of the sixth line 'so Hsiao Hsiang'; and a combination of rhyme and alliteration at the beginning of the second line 'yü yü'. But looking further into the poem there will be found to be more complicated patterns—such as the second line's internal alliteration of the second character 'yü' with the last character 'yang', and the internal rhyming in that line of 'fang' with 'yang', and with 'ch'ang' in the first line.

For onomatopoeia reference has already been made to Chiang Chieh's Poem (No. 67)—see the last line of the first verse for the noise of rain 'Hsiao hsiao'. Yüeh Fei uses the same sound in the second line of his poem (No. 56).

This collection of poems covers a period of roughly a thousand years. They have been picked as the best in that long time and are all well-known to the Chinese. The great majority are available in Chinese in one popular anthology or another. (We have only been able to trace about half in English published translations.) Li Yü of the Southern T'ang Dynasty comes in for special attention in the collection because his writing, particularly after his captivity, comes so true to us across the years. A large proportion are from the Sung Dynasty poets for it was they who brought the tz'u to its peak of excellence.

There is no escape from the general difficulty of appreciating Chinese poetry of other ages without some knowledge of the historical and social conditions ruling at the time the verses were written. One is faced then with a dilemma. Is the English verse to be 'explained' with notes and appendices? Or is the reader to be left unfettered to put his own interpretation on it even if this misses something of what was likely to have been in the poet's mind?

We have attempted to steer a middle course, presenting the poems first, and placing this note and appendices at the back of the book. With this minimum of assistance the reader will be left, it is hoped, not with a picture of inscrutability and of an alien culture, but rather with the impression of warmly human men and women who expressed their pleasures and their yearnings in a language common to them all over the centuries and formidably alive today.

# APPENDIX I

## A Brief Historical Background to the T'zu

*The earliest tz'u in this collection date from the T'ang Dynasty (Li Po—701–762 A.D.). But as references are made in some of these poems to earlier times this brief historical background begins with the Ch'in Dynasty (221–206 B.C).*

| Dynasty and Date | | Poets (of this collection) |
|---|---|---|
| CH'IN 221–206 B.C. | The old feudal system of ancient China was abolished and the Empire first unified under Ch'in Shih Huang Ti. The Great Wall was completed. A single unified written character system was brought in over the whole empire. The classical and historical books were burnt to abolish 'feudalism' and stifle criticism of the Emperor's reforms. The capital was established at Hsien-yang in Shensi province. | |
| HAN 206 B.C.–220 A.D. | The revolution started by the Ch'in Dynasty was forwarded and consolidated by Liu Pang, the founder of the Han Dynasty, and there followed great expansion and consolidation of the Empire. The southern provinces (Kwangsi and Kwangtung) and Central Asian tracts (Sin-kiang) were incorporated after contact had been made even further west, as far as Turkestan. Ch'ang-an (near Hsien-yang) was set up as the capital, and was to remain as such until the Sung Dynasty. The making of rag paper and early types of porcelain were invented. Literature and the arts flourished. | |

THREE
KINGDOMS
(*San Kuo*) 220–317 A.D.    A period of internecine battles followed—since popularised through legend and the theatre.

*There now followed, from 317 A.D. to the establishment of the Republic in the present century, a succession of foreign invasions by either Central Asian Turk, Tartar, Mongol or Tungusic peoples from the north-west and north, alternating with periods when the Chinese regained control of part or the whole of the Empire.*

| *Dynasty and Date* | | *Poets* |
|---|---|---|
| (IN NORTH CHINA) TARTARS 317–550 A.D. | Hsiung Nu, Hsien P'ei, and Wei (T'o-pa) Tartar tribes over-ran the north part of the Empire, but gradually became assimilated. The Northern Han capital, Ch'ang-an was sacked, and the Imperial library at Loyang burnt. A great impetus was thereby given to the migration south of enormous numbers of Chinese, including many scholars. | |
| (IN SOUTH CHINA) SIX DYNASTIES 317–589 A.D. | This period of the Six Dynasties covered a series of Chinese rulers, starting with the Chin and ending with the Ch'en dynasty. Their capital Chin-ling (Nanking) on the Yangtze River became a gay and prosperous city. | |
| SUI 589–618 A.D. | The Empire was reunified by a Chinese general, Yang Chien, who founded the short-lived Sui Dynasty. | |
| T'ANG 618–907 A.D. | The T'ang Dynasty was established chiefly as the result of a brilliant Chinese commander, scholar and administrator, Li Shih Min, and led to nearly 300 years of expansion and consolidation with only one brief interlude of revolt by An Lu Shan, a Tartar General, in the reign of Emperor Hsüan Tsung (Ming Huang). The Capital, Ch'ang-an, was rebuilt, and the Tartars subdued. The art of printing was invented; sculpture, painting, and literature flourished; and in particular | LI PO PO CHÜ I WEN T'ING YÜN |

the lyric (tz'u) form of poetry was developed. Contact over long land-routes was established with the west, as far as the Byzantine Empire. A centralised government was set up with officials selected by merit through a classical examination system. The dynasty finally broke up as a result of a revolt of its army in the South.

FIVE DYNASTIES PERIOD 907–959 A.D.

In this period the Empire was split up into separate kingdoms under warring rulers (of these the one that is most concerned in this collection of poems is the kingdom of 'Southern T'ang', two of whose three rulers are represented here).

LI YING (NAN T'ANG CHUNG CHU)
LI YÜ (NAN TANG HOU CHU)

SUNG 960–1126 A.D.

The Sung Dynasty was founded by the Chinese general Chao K'uang Yin, who re-unified the empire. Negotiation and compromise were more evident than force. Khitan Tartar tribes gained a foothold in north-eastern China and set up their capital at Yen (now Peking). The arts flourished greatly. Nü-chen Tartars over-ran the Khitans first, and then captured the Sung capital of Pien-liang, taking two Emperors (father and son) into captivity.

FAN CHUNG YEN
YEH CH'ING CHEN
YEN SHU
YEN CHI TAO
OU YANG HSIU
LIU YUNG
SU SHIH
HUANG T'ING CHIEN
CH'IN KUAN
CHOU PANG YEN
LI CH'ING CHAO

SOUTHERN SUNG 1127–1278 A.D.

The younger son of the Sung captive Emperor fled south and as Emperor Kao Tsung, established the Southern Sung Dynasty, setting up his capital in Hangchow. Nü-chen Tartars, after they had pushed south and sacked Yangchow and other cities, were eventually held by the Sung Army under General Yüeh Fei (the writer of poem No. 56 in this collection), roughly on the line of the Huai River.

YÜEH FEI
LU YU
HSIN CH'I CHI
CHIANG K'UEI
LIU K'O CHUANG
WU WEN YING
CHIANG CHIEH

A policy of appeasement was adopted by Southern Sungs and no attempt was made to regain control of northern China from the Tartars.

| | | |
|---|---|---|
| (IN NORTH CHINA) CHIN (NÜ CHEN TARTARS) 1115–1234 A.D. | Nüchen Tartars established themselves in North China as the Chin Dynasty. | |
| YÜAN (MONGOL) 1206–1368 A.D. | Genghiz Khan first put pressure on the Nüchen Tartars (Chin Dynasty) in 1206 A.D. but he then turned his attention to Central Asia and the West. His successors in 1234 attacked the Chin northern capital and in 1276 eventually captured the Southern Sung capital of Hangchow. Kublai Khan set up a unified Chinese Empire in 1280. The Mongol invasion was carried out with the utmost ferocity and savagery, resulting incidentally in a great southward migration of Chinese. The Chinese Empire's boundaries—in this Yüan (Mongol) Dynasty—were pushed south and west to include Burma, Assam and Tibet, but there was failure to capture Japan and Cambodia. Chinese opposition gradually gathered force as the Mongol rulers deteriorated. | SA TU LA LIU CHI (PO WEN) |
| MING 1368–1644 | The Mongols were overthrown and the Ming Dynasty established by a Chinese general Chu Yüan Chang, and the period became famous as one of expansion, both geographically and of the arts—particularly the drama. The capital was transferred from Nanking to Peking. A series of short-lived Emperors and consequent misgovernment led to delegation of power into the hands of the Palace eunuchs and the undermining of the dynasty. | LIU CHI (PO WEN) |
| CH'ING (MANCHU) 1644–1911 | The Manchus, successors to the Tartar tribes (Khitans and Nü-chens), were invited by the Mings to suppress a rebellion, but themselves took over | NA-LAN HSING-TE TSO FU |

control of the whole country. However they slowly became softened by life in China, and there followed a closing in of the empire on itself by discouragement of intercourse with outside powers. After leading the world over a period of 1500 years, with such inventions as paper-making, porcelain, gunpowder, the wheelbarrow, the compass and printing, China was left behind in the technological advance in the West.

*It is no part of this collection of lyrics—the last of which was written in about 1800—to comment on the epoch-making revolutions of this century, the repercussions of which are still in progress.*

# APPENDIX II

## Notes on Poems

*Poem*
*Number*

### LI PO

2. *Line 6.* 'Lê-yu-yüan' was a vantage point of high flat ground (in the south-east corner of the T'ang capital, Ch'ang-an) giving a commanding view.
   *Line 9.* The west wind was a chill wind.
3. *Verse 2, line 4.* See 'Note on the Tz'u', p. 218.

### PO CHÜ I

5. *Lines 1 and 2.* The Pien and Ssu rivers were near the city of Pien-liang (later to become the capital of the Sung Dynasty and now known as K'ai-feng). Their waters were connected to the east with the Grand Canal, and therefore flowed south eventually to the Yangtze river, on which Kua-chou was a ferry-point.

### WEN T'ING YÜN

6. (i) *Line 3.* The 'water-clock', or clepsydra, consisted of a series of water-containers on descending levels, dripping water from one into the next below (on the same principle as sand through an hour-glass); the time was measured in the lowest container on a bamboo stick, which rose as the water filled.
   (ii) *Line 9.* 'Hsieh domain.' The Hsieh family in the time of the Chin Dynasty was noted for its wealth and large possessions.

### NAN T'ANG CHUNG CHU (LI YING)

7. *Verse 2, line 1.* Orioles were regarded as migratory birds capable of carrying messages for those who could interpret their notes. (See also Huang T'ing Chien, Poem 48.)

*Verse 2, line 3.* There is an alternative version of the sixth character in this line, meaning 'gorges, ravines' rather than 'Ch'u' (i.e. places in the old State of Ch'u)—as written in the Chinese here. In the context it would appear that the poet was referring to (three) places on the river, in the State of Ch'u, where the water was turbulent, i.e. ravines or gorges.

8. (i) *Verse 2, line 1.* 'The Cock Fort.' The two characters in the Chinese (Chi Sai) can be variously translated. A likely interpretation, bearing in mind that this line and the next form a pair, would seem to be that Li Ying was referring either to the frontier post Chi-lu-sai (now known as Heng-shan in Shensi Province) on the Great Wall 'far away' (as his dream carried him); or—if one can discount the force of the character 'Yüan' meaning 'far'—to Chi-kung-p'o, the Cock Fort, one of the two forts protecting his capital Chin-ling (now known as Nanking). Li Ying, as independent ruler of the Southern T'angs, decided to throw in his lot, as a vassal, with the powerful Chao K'uang Yin, the founder of the Sung Dynasty. Having done this he might well look back with nostalgia to the many times he must have visited this fort where it stood as an emblem of his independence.

    (ii) *Verse 2, line 2.* The musical instrument, the sheng, referred to here was a type of large mouth-organ. It consisted of an air-container, originally made of a gourd but later of heavier material. Air was blown into it through a tube, and the sound produced through a series of copper-reeded bamboo pipes set into the top of the air-container and provided with holes to vary the notes with the fingers. (There is an excellent illustration of sheng being played, in the *New Oxford History of Music*, Vol. I, Plate IV.)

## NAN T'ANG HOU CHU (LI YÜ)

### PRE-CAPTIVITY POEMS (NOS. 9–16)

9. These two verses are in fact separate poems written to a tune of five lines' length. However as they form a pair—about spring and autumn—they have been printed together here.

    (i) *Verse 1, line 5.* 'And anxious eyes that watch earth's blossoming.' See 'Note on the Tz'u', p. 217.

    (ii) *Verse 2, line 3.* There is an alternative version of this line, often printed, quoting the last character as 'evening' as opposed to 'distant' (which is the same character as that which ends the first line of this verse). If this alternative were to be adopted this line would read 'Endless miles of river and hills in cold evening colours'.

10. This poem is considered to have been written by Li Yü about his first Queen, a woman of great charm and ability.

   While the poem starts, according to some anthologies, with the character meaning 'evening' instead of 'morning', and though the former would seem to be the more natural setting for this scene, we have held to 'morning' as the more authoritative text.

11. *Line 3.* 'and chill slap of sodden cloth on stone.' The thud as women beat out their clothes to wash them clean, especially along a river or canal bank, is a very common sound in China.

12. This poem was probably written, like the following one, about the Queen's young sister with whom the King was having an affair.

   (i) *Verse 1, line 1.* The first line refers to the copper-reeded bamboo tubes of the 'sheng'. (For 'sheng' see Poem No. 8, note (ii).)

   (ii) *Verse 2, line 1.* 'Yü yün', literally meaning 'rain (and) cloud', was the literary term for sexual intercourse.

13. As in the case of the previous poem (No. 12) this describes a clandestine meeting between the Queen's young sister and the King.

15. *Verse 1, line 4.* The 'Rainbow Skirt' was a well-known tune.

16. Tradition has it that Li Yü was composing this poem when the Sung troops were surrounding his capital Chin-ling (now Nanking). It is held by scholars that the last three lines of the complete poem to this p'u had not been written when the city fell and that Li Yü left it incomplete; the Chinese version here accordingly stops short at the seventh line. Three last lines are however often printed in some anthologies and though they were probably not written by Li Yü, we have translated a version of them here to round the poem off in the English.

### POST-CAPTIVITY POEMS (NOS. 17–27)

18. *Line 7.* 'Rivers flow east for ever . . .' See 'Note on the Tz'u', p. 218. See also Poem 25, last line.

19. (i) *Line 2.* The Chinese literally refers to the moon as being 'like a hook'. But the word 'bow' is also applied to the moon, in this context the waxing moon being referred to as an 'upward bow' and the waning moon a 'downward bow'.

   (ii) *Line 3.* 'Phoenix branches' were, in the literal Chinese, the wu t'ung trees, of which the scientific name is Firmiana simplex (L.) Wight. There was a saying (see Matthew's *Chinese-English*

*Dictionary*) that this was the only tree on the branches of which the legendary bird, the phoenix, would rest; hence it is sometimes known as the Phoenix Tree. But the name 'wu t'ung' is likely to have been applied to more than one tree species. Both a Paulownia and a Catalpa species are liable to be referred to today in Peking as 'wu t'ung' trees.

(iii) *Line 7*. A more literal rendering of the last line would read 'It leaves behind an after-taste the heart will know'.

22. *Verse 2, line 1*. 'The wild geese have flown in yet there's no trace of news.' See 'Note on the Tz'u', p. 219.

23. (i) *Verse 2, line 1*. This line could either be read 'Alone, (I) must not lean on the railing' or 'Alone, in the evening, (I) lean on the railing', according as to which of the two alternative meanings 'not/don't' or 'evening' of mo/mu is used.

(ii) *Verse 2, line 5*. The Chinese line of four characters literally means 'Heaven above man among'. The flowing of rivers, the fading of flowers, and the passing of spring are nature's phenomena, regular and immutable, and as regularly recreated. But in this world man cannot put the clock back and his separation from his past is as complete as heaven above from the earth of men.

24. (i) *Verse 2, line 1*. In some anthologies—possibly more authoritative—this line does not refer to the putting away of his sword but of his life of pleasure. In view however of the following line we have chosen the text containing the character for 'sword'.

(ii) *Verse 2, line 5*. The Ch'in Huai was a small water-way running through Chin-ling (now Nanking) past the Palace walls down to the Yangtze River.

25. This poem is said to have cost Li Yü his life. The Sung Emperor, T'ai Tsung, probably irritated by Li Yü's hankering for his past independence, is said to have had him poisoned, on the grounds that the third line of this poem furnished confirmation that Li Yü was planning a rebellion in his old domain.

*Verse 2, line 4*. 'My heart's a river . . . that must for ever eastwards flow.' See 'Note on the Tz'u', p. 218.

27. (i) *Verse 1, lines 3–4*. In this song-pattern it was prescribed that the third and fourth lines should 'pair' (see 'Note on the Tz'u', p. 224), and this ornamentation has been reflected in the English verse.

(ii) *Verse 2, line 2*. Both 'Shen' and 'P'an' are literary allusions to two traditional characters, the one Shen Yüeh of the Liu Sung Dynasty who became hunch-backed, and the other P'an An Jen whose hair went white in his youth.

## FAN CHUNG YEN

28. (i) *Verse 1, line 2.* The Chinese in this line refers specifically to the Heng Yang range of hills as the place to which the geese were flying. These hills, in Hunan province, were traditionally regarded as the point where the geese wintered, remaining there until they returned north the following spring. (See 'Note on the Tz'u', p. 218.)

(ii) *Verse 2, line 2.* 'We have gained no glory here.' The Chinese here literally means '(We have) cut no (memorial) in the Yen Jan (hills)', this being the scene of an earlier conquest in the far north-west. In the Han Dynasty in about A.D. 90 Tou Hsien, with the famous general Pan Ch'ao as his deputy, defeated the Hsiung Nu here, and commemorated his victory by engraving a memorial in the Yen Jan hills.

(iii) *Verse 2, line 3.* 'The tribal pipes.' The Chinese here refers to the 'Ch'iang pipes', the Ch'iang being a well-known frontier tribe living on the high grass-lands near the Tibetan border.

## YEN SHU

33. *Verse 1, line 2.* 'And its Ch'ing Ming time . . .' Ch'ing Ming was the spring festival—at about our Easter-time—when the Chinese paid their respects at the family graves.

## YEN CHI TAO

34. (i) *Verse 2, line 1.* The Chinese refers specifically to the girl's name 'Hsiao P'in', that is 'Little Water-plant'.

(ii) *Verse 2, line 2.* ' "Heart" had been embroidered on both the silks she wore.' It was, and still is, a common practice to have Chinese characters, such as those for 'happiness', 'long life',—and as in this case for 'heart'—woven into or embroidered on material for clothes.

## OU YANG HSIU

35. This poem is also attributed to the poetess Chu Shu Chen.

*Verse 1, line 1.* The Lantern Festival took place on the 15th day of the 1st month (Chinese calendar).

36. (i) *Verse 2, line 1.* It was not considered unmanly for him to wear a flower; what might be laughable was that he should go to the trouble of wearing a flower with no black hair to show it off.

(ii) *Verse 2, line 2.* The 'Lu Yao' was the name of a well-known tune with a fast rhythm.

37. *Verse 1, line 2.* The 'Plum' style hair display might have been the practice of putting plum-blossom in the hair. (See Appendix II, Note on Poem 64 (ii).)
38. (i) In this song pattern it is prescribed that the fifth and sixth lines (the first two of the second verse) should form a 'pair', (see 'Note on the Tz'u', page 224 'Parallelism'), and this has been reflected in the English verse.

    (ii) *Verse 2, line 4.* The Mandarin duck and drake symbolized married happiness.
39. *Verse 2, line 4.* The Chinese, in this line, refers to 'crystal' pillows. In the Imperial Palace Museum in Peking there is a white porcelain pillow (Sung Dynasty), of the kind which could well have been in the poet's mind.
40. This is usually considered to be a 'political' poem; the poet pictures himself as a recluse, out of favour, while the 'rich and gay', small men and busy-bodies, have the ear of the Emperor.

    *Verse 1, line 5.* The 'Pavilion of Display' is a literary reference to the courtesans' quarter.

## LIU YUNG

41. (i) *Verse 1, line 11.* ' . . . as vast as under Southern skies.' The Chinese of this line refers to the skies of 'Ch'u', that is one of the Southern ancient states (about 500 B.C.) lying roughly in the present Hunan and Hupeh Provinces, a country of lakes, rivers and distant horizons.

    (ii) *Verse 2, line 4.* 'By a willow-bank, a wind at dawn, the moon upon the wane.' See the biographical note on Su Shih, p. 111, contrasting this line with one of Su Shih's.

## SU SHIH

42. *Verse 2, line 3.* 'Chiang-nan' was the province near the lower reaches of the Yangtze River now roughly covered by the provinces of Kiangsu and Anhwei and well-known to Su Shih, who was at one time Governor of Hangchow.
43. This tz'u is considered by some to be a 'political' poem in which the poet refers to himself as a recluse, out of favour with the Emperor. Others consider that he is referring to a girl who followed him about, entranced by his poetry reading; and who died far from her home.
44. Su Shih records that he based this poem on one he had heard recited in his youth, composed by Meng Ch'ang, ruler of the Later Shu Kingdom, in about the tenth century A.D. In fact

what purports to be Meng Ch'ang's original poem has come down to us, shorter than Su Shih's, similar but inferior to it.

45. This tz'u was written by Su Shih, thinking of his brother. Su Shih himself was temporarily out of favour in Court circles and had been transferred from the capital to a minor provincial post.

46. This poem is about the Red Cliff (Ch'ih Pi) on the Yangtze River—the 'great river' of the opening line—in what is now Hupeh Province. This is famous in history, legend, and drama as the place where Chou Yü, a general of the Wu Kingdom, defeated the great Ts'ao Ts'ao of the Wei Kingdom by burning his fleet of junks. This period of China's history, where legend has filled in what the record lacked, is known as that of the Three Kingdoms (third century A.D.), that is the kingdoms of Wei, Wu, and Shu. A highly coloured story of the times was written by Lo Kuan Chung in the Ming Dynasty—the San Kuo Chih Yen I—and is extremely well-known from adaptations on the Chinese stage.

    Chou Yü whose sovereign was Sun Ch'üan (also called Sun Chung Mou—see Hsin Ch'i Chi's Poem No. 60 on p. 165) was married to the younger (the Hsiao Ch'iao or Little Ch'iao of this poem) of two beautiful sisters, the elder having been married to Sun Ts'e, Sun Ch'üan's father. The story has it that Chou Yü would not have recommended to his ruler that Ts'ao Ts'ao be opposed at all had not an astute ally let fall the remark that Ts'ao Ts'ao's real object in invading the Kingdom of Wu was to carry off the two Ch'iao sisters.

    The story goes on to say that Ts'ao Ts'ao had advanced south from his northern Kingdom of Wei and encamped on the Yangtze river by the Red Cliff. He had amassed a large fleet of junks to transport his army down the river for his attack on the Kingdom of Wu. His troops were not used to the rough conditions which can be experienced on a river as broad as the Yangtze, and he was persuaded by a planted deserter to make fast his junks in large blocks so as to steady them. While his enemy was downwind there was not normally, at that time of the year, any danger of an attack by fire ships. But Chou Yü seized the opportunity of a change in the wind, launched fire ships disguised as friendly vessels, and wiped out Ts'ao Ts'ao's fleet.

47. This tz'u is an 'Ode to the Willow Flower' based on his friend Chang Chih Fu's poem on the same subject.

    *Verse 2, line 5.* 'The pond a mass of duck-weed drift!' There was an old saying that willow-down which fell on to water changed into duck-weed, neither apparently having any root.

## HUANG T'ING CHIEN

48. *Verse 2.* 'From the oriole's mouth . . . a myriad warbling notes nobody understands.' See Appendix Note on Poem No. 7 (p. 232).
49. (i) For a note on the rhyming and alliteration in this tz'u see 'Note on the Tz'u', p. 225.
    (ii) *Verse 2, line 2.* 'Clouds on the painted screen mantle the Hsiao and Hsiang.' The Hsiao and Hsiang rivers pictured on the screen are the site of a legend about two sisters, both married to the virtuous Emperor Shun, one of the two father-figures of the perfect ruler (the other being the Emperor Yao). These two sisters O Huang and Nü Ying were given to the Emperor Shun in 2288 B.C. and were models of faithfulness. They were on a journey with the Emperor when he died in Ts'ang Wu, and when he was buried there by the river Hsiang the two sisters' tears flowed so unceasingly that the bamboo leaves became, and continued to grow, spotted.

## CH'IN KUAN

50. (i) For a piece of music associated with this tz'u see 'Note on the Tz'u', pp. 219/220.
    (ii) *Line 5.* The last three Chinese characters literally mean 'Deep close door(s)' which imply not that one door was to be well-closed but that several doors, 'in depth' in a series of courtyards, were to be shut.
51. *Verse 2, lines 1–3.* The poet is being given a parting present, which took the form of the girl's perfume sachet; this was usually attached to the girdle. It was not unknown for a man going off for a long separation to carry about such a reminder of his loved one, and there is a story of one young man who did this only to find that his prospective father-in-law, who had not been made a party to the scheme, recognized the scent.

    The girdle itself was also a symbol of conjugal happiness—and separation was sometimes spoken of as a 'loosening of the girdle'.

## CHOU PANG YEN

52. (i) See 'Note on the Tz'u', p. 216.
    *Verse 1, line 1.* 'Ping' was a district noted for its knives and swords.

(ii) *Verse 1, line 3.* The Orange was an imported rarity at that time.

(iii) *Verse 1, line 6.* For 'sheng' see Appendix, Note on Poem No. 8, p. 233.

53. This is one of the occasions when a poet indicated the subject of his lyric—in this case 'A Red Rose'.

(i) *Verse 2, line 2.* The poet has represented spring by the Red Rose, 'the matchless joy of the Ch'u Palace'. The Chinese of this line is literally 'Bury Ch'u Palace overthrow kingdom'; the last two words are an allusion to a concubine who was introduced to the Emperor Wu of the Han Dynasty as a beauty from whom 'one glance would overthrow a city, and two a kingdom', in other words of 'devastating beauty'.

(ii) *Verse 3, lines 8–11.* It was not uncommon for a man to put a flower in his hair (see Note on Poem No. 36, Verse 2, line 1, p. 236) while a woman might go further in transfixing a big blossom with a hair-pin, which would therefore 'bend in grace' and quiver as if 'bowing . . . to passers by'.

(iii) *Verse 3, last two lines.* There was a superstition that the fallen blossom, if one could only interpret any figure in its centre which faintly resembled a Chinese character, might carry a message.

## LI CH'ING CHAO

54. (i) *Verse 1, line 3.* The Ch'ung Yang Festival fell towards the end of autumn when chrysanthemums were in flower.

(ii) *Verse 2, line 1.* The three characters translated as 'at the eastern hedge' are taken from a poem by T'ao Ch'ien

'Gathering chrysanthemums by the eastern hedge
While I leisurely gaze at the southern hills.'

## YÜEH FEI

56. (i) *Line 1.* The opening four characters of this poem meaning 'So angry that my hair bristled to the extent of lifting my hat' were first attributed to the behaviour of a great minister, Lin Hsiang Ju of the Chao Kingdom in the third century B.C., during negotiations he was having with the aggressive Ch'in Kingdom.

(ii) *Line 10.* Ching K'ang was the reign title assumed by the Emperor Ch'in Tsung who, with his father Wei Tsung, was taken into captivity by the Nüchen Tartars when they captured the Sung capital in A.D. 1126.

(iii) *Line 12.* The 'Palace Men' were the appeasers, headed by the Prime Minister Ch'in Kuei, who wished to come to terms with the 'Barbarians' rather than fight.

(iv) *Line 15.* Ho Lan Shan, the stronghold of the Tartars in the north.

LU YU

57. *Verse 1, line 1.* This opening line can be variously translated. The meaning chosen here for the Chinese words 'Red (or pink) flaky (or crisp) hands' is that they refer to the northern shortbread, shaped in the making to look like a man's hand.

HSIN CH'I CHI

59. (i) *Verse 1, line 1.* This line refers to the custom of a woman's breaking a hairpin into two, giving one half as a parting present or a special reminder of a pact.

(ii) *Verse 1, lines 2-3.* The Chinese in line 2 is an allusion to a ferry-point near Nanking called after T'ao-yeh (Peach Leaf) a concubine of Wang Hsien Chih (third century A.D.). The name came to mean a point at which partings took place, as did 'Nan-p'u' in the following line of this poem.

60. (i) *Verse 1, line 3.* Sun Chung Mou was a sovereign ruler of the Wu Kingdom in the period of the Three Kingdoms—see Appendix II, Note on Poem No. 46.

(ii) *Verse 1, lines 8-11, and verse 2, line 2.* The vigorous attitude of the Emperor Chi-Nu of the Liu Sung Dynasty, and of the Han General Huo Ch'ü Ping who defeated the Hsiung Nu Barbarians at Lang Chü Hsü is contrasted with the weak behaviour of the Southern Sung Government, which is likened to that of the 'muddled' reign of the Emperor Yüan Chia.

(iii) *Verse 2, lines 11-12.* General Lien Po, one of the two great men of the Chao Kingdom in the third century B.C., (the other being the Chief Minister Lin Hsiang Ju, see p. 240) was a man of phenomenal appetite. On one occasion, some time after the General had retired, the Emperor, desperate for a good Commander in the field, sent a special envoy to see him. As a guide to judge the General's fitness to take on the task, the envoy was simply asked to see whether his appetite was as good as ever.

61. (i) *Verse 2, lines 1-7.* Hsin Ch'i Chi who finds himself kept away from the capital and from being able to exert any influence towards a policy of aggression against the Tartars in the north—as opposed to the existing policy of the appeasers at Court—

likens his predicament to that of Han Wu Ti's Empress Ch'en who was kept virtually imprisoned and incommunicado behind 'The Long Door' in the Palace. She was eventually restored to the Emperor's favour as a result of an appeal to him which she commissioned the famous prose-writer Ssu-ma Hsiang-ju (see line 4 as 'Hsiang-ju') to submit on her behalf. But Hsin Ch'i Chi feels he would awaken no sympathy even if he achieved such a reconciliation. However he suggests the Ministers—the appeasers—should remember they are not there permanently, and will pass away just as two famous palace women did in their day, Yü Huan (the childhood name of Yang Kuei Fei, the favourite concubine of the T'ang Emperor Hsüan Tsung) and Chao Fei Yen (a concubine, later raised to the status of Empress Consort, of the Emperor Cheng in the first century B.C.).

(ii) *Verse 2, last three lines.* It was to the north-west, where the sun set, that the Tartars were entrenched, having set themselves up in the old capital.

## CHIANG K'UEI

62. See Biographical Note, p. 169.
 *Verse 1, line 6.* Ho Hsün lived in the sixth century A.D.; he was famous for his verse on 'plum-blossom'.
63. This tz'u is a lament for the town of Yangchow sacked by the Tartars some twenty years before the poet was born.

(i) *Verse 1, line 1.* Yangchow lay on the north bank of the Yangtze river, east of a trunk road which ran north to the Huai River.

(ii) *Verse 1, line 2.* Chu-hsi (literally 'West of the Bamboos') was a beauty spot near Yangchow at which a pavilion had been built (Chu-hsi-t'ing), but we have held in the English version to the transliterated form of the place-name.

(iii) *Verse 2, line 1.* The poet Tu Mu was very fond of Yangchow and wrote later:
'I was ten years awakening from a Yangchow dream
Though all I earned was a reputation for feckless behaviour in the Azure Tower' (i.e., the courtesans' quarter).

(iv) *Verse 2, line 10.* One of the twenty-four bridges is said to have been called the 'Red Bridge' after the flowers that grew there.

64. (i) *Lines 7–8.* Refers to Wang Chao Chün, a famous beauty in the Palace of the Han Emperor Yüan. As part of the provisions of a peace-treaty with the Hsiung-nu Tartars in the north-west, the Emperor bestowed her upon the Tartar Khan.

A colourful legend about the whole incident was dramatized, and in this play Wang Chao Chün is so unhappy in her Tartar life that she commits suicide by throwing herself into a river.

(ii) *Lines 11–13.* These lines refer to the story that plum blossom settled on the Princess Shou Yang while she was asleep in the Palace, and that as a result she introduced the custom of putting flowers in the hair.

(iii) *Line 16.* 'A golden room.' This refers to the remark by Han Wu Ti, when he was still a boy, on being asked by his mother whether he would like to marry the beautiful Ah Chiao. He would be so pleased, he said, that he would build a golden room for her. (For his subsequent treatment of this girl after she became the Empress Ch'en, see Appendix II, Poem 61, p. 242.)

WU WEN YING

66. (i) *Verse 1, line 1.* 'Ch'ing Ming.' See Appendix Note, Poem 33, p. 236.

(ii) *Verse 2, line 6.* 'Mandarin ducks.' See Appendix, Note on Poem 38, p. 237.

CHIANG CHIEH

67. (i) *Verse 1, line 4.* A T'ang Dynasty Governor Li Te Yü had a famous concubine called Hsieh Ch'iu Niang (which might be translated Autumn Beauty Hsieh) and the name Ch'iu Niang became very common. T'ai Niang was another common girl's name and there would be hundreds of bridges and fords called after them.

(ii) *Verse 2, line 2.* Though the word 'flute' is used here the musical instrument was in fact the 'sheng'—see Note on Poem No. 8, p. 233.

SA TU LA

68. *Verse 1, line 3.* Sa Tu La is writing of the past glories of the Six Dynasties period (A.D. 317–589). Previous to this, the country in the lower reaches of the Yangtze river was famous (in the sixth century B.C.) as the Wu and Ch'u Kingdoms.

See also Note on Poem No. 69 below.

69. A tz'u written about the past glories of Chin-ling (now known as Nanking) the capital at the time of the Six Dynasties (A.D. 317–589). With the unification of the Empire the capital was

transferred to the north and Chin-ling's prosperity and glamour faded.

(i) *Verse 1, lines 7–8*. The Wang and Hsieh families were famous as litterateurs. Though there was a lapse of at least 700 years between these families' prosperity and Sa Tu La's writing of this poem, and though the buildings would have gone, the street might still have been known as Blackcoat Lane.

(ii) *Verse 2, lines 7–8*. The allusion to the 'Well of Shame'—literally in Chinese 'the Powder Well' in this rendering, but there is an alternative version meaning 'The Well of Humiliation'—is to an incident in the period of the Six Dynasties. On hearing of the arrival of the Sui soldiery at the gates of the Imperial Palace the debauched last Emperor of the Ch'en Dynasty gave the order that he himself and two imperial concubines should be lowered into a well, where they were later discovered. They were dragged out, the Emperor's life being spared.

## NA-LAN HSING-TE

71. *Verse 1, line 3*. The Yü Kuan Pass is the point where the Great Wall comes down to the sea, separating the old China from Manchuria, and is now known as Shan-hai-kuan.
72. *Verse 2, lines 1–2*. There are two allusions to legends here. The first is to the man who fell in love with the beautiful Yün Ying. He was told that if he drank liquid jade (i.e. jade hammered into a powder) he would meet her at the Blue Bridge, where the Cave of the Immortals was to be found.

    The second allusion—to reaching heaven by magic—is to a figure in Chinese mythology, Ch'ang O. Her husband, Shen I, was given the Pill of Immortality, and hid it in the rafters of his house. There Ch'ang O found it, and swallowing it was wafted up to the moon where she lived in a splendid palace.

## TSO FU

73. In Po Chü I's original poem, to which this tz'u alludes, a host (the 'way-worn passer-by' in Tso Fu's tz'u) and his guest going down to the river one evening, are entranced by the sound of a guitar coming from a near-by boat. The player turns out to be a girl who is persuaded to join them and tell her story. She describes how, after becoming one of the best p'i p'a (guitar) players and most sought-after courtesans in the capital, she falls on bad times, then marries a merchant but finds herself spending a lonely life of separation.

# APPENDIX III

## Tune-Patterns

Showing the numbers of characters in each line
of the Chinese text

As previously mentioned in the Preface and Note on the Tz'u, the Chinese text of each of the poems in this collection is written in the traditional form without indicating the length of individual lines by punctuation marks. (Where they wish to do so the Chinese leave a gap to indicate the end of a stanza.) The following table sets out the 'pattern' of the poem for each tune-title, showing in the right-hand column consecutively the numbers of characters in each line.

Just as there are varying texts of many of these poems, so the pattern of the tune-titles can be variously represented in different anthologies; in the latter case the differences are usually minor ones of punctuation, which is almost always included in the printing of modern editions. No attempt has been made here to set out an authoritative 'standard' pattern for each tune-title. The object of this Appendix is rather to indicate the pattern and punctuation as the translator saw it, so that the two versions of Chinese and English can the more readily be compared.

With this explanation and reference table it is hoped that the decision to write the Chinese text in the traditional way without punctuation, thereby making the most pleasing picture of each poem, will be as acceptable to the foreign reader as it will undoubtedly be to the Chinese.

| Poem Number | Poet | P'u (tune-title) | Pattern (characters in each line) |
|---|---|---|---|
| 1 | Li Po | Ch'ing P'ing Tiao | 7-7-7-7 |
| 2 | ,, ,, | I Ch'in O | 3-7-3-4-4; 7-7-3-4-4 |
| 3 | ,, ,, | P'u Sa Man | 7-7-5-5; 5-5-5-5 |
| 4 | Po Chü I | Hua Fei Hua | 3-3-3-3-7-7 |
| 5 | ,, ,, ,, | Ch'ang Hsiang Ssu | 3-3-7-5; 3-3-7-5 |
| 6 | Wen T'ing Yün | Keng Lou Tzu | 3-3-6-3-5; 3-3-6-3-3-5 |
| 7 | Nan T'ang Chung Chu (Li Ying) | T'an P'o Wan Ch'i Sha | 7-7-3; 7-7-3 |
| 8 | ,, ,, | ,, | (See Poem No. 7) |
| 9 | Nan T'ang Hou Chu (Li Yü) | Wang Chiang Mei | 3-5-7-7-5 |
| 10 | ,, | I Ho Chu | 4-7-7-4-5; 7-7-7-4-5 |
| 11 | ,, | Tao Lien Tzu Chin | 3-3-7-7-7 |
| 12 | ,, | P'u Sa Man | (See Poem No. 3) |
| 13 | ,, | ,, | (See Poem No. 3) |
| 14 | ,, | Hsi Ch'ien Ying | 3-3-5-7-5; 3-3-6-7-5 |
| 15 | ,, | Yü Lou Ch'un | 7-7-7-7; 7-7-7-7 |
| 16 | ,, | Lin Chiang Hsien | 7-6-7-4-5; 7-6-7-4-5 |
| 17 | ,, | Wang Chiang Nan | 3-5-7-7-5 (See also Wang-Chiang Mei, Poem No. 9) |
| 18 | ,, | Wu Yeh T'i | 6-3-6-3-3-3-6-3 |
| 19 | ,, | ,, | (See Poem No. 18) |
| 20 | ,, | Wan Ch'i Sha | 7-7-7; 7-7-7 |
| 21 | ,, | Tzu Yeh Ko | 7-7-5-5; 5-5-5-5 (See P'u Sa Man, Poem No. 3) |
| 22 | ,, | Ch'ing P'ing Le | 4-5-7-6; 6-6-6-6 |
| 23 | ,, | Lang T'ao Sha | 5-4-7-7-4; 5-4-7-7-4 |
| 24 | ,, | ,, | (See Poem No. 23) |
| 25 | ,, | Yü Mei Jen | 7-5-7-9; 7-5-7-9 |

| Poem Number | Poet | P'u (tune-title) | Pattern (characters in each line) |
|---|---|---|---|
| 26 | ,, | ,, ,, | 7-5-7-6-3; 7-5-7-6-3 |
| 27 | ,, | P'o Chen Tzu | 6-6-7-7-5; 6-6-7-7-5 |
| 28 | Fan Chung Yen | Yü Chia Ao | 7-7-7-3-7; 7-7-7-3-7 |
| 29 | ,, | Su Mu Che | 3-3-4-5-7-4-5; 3-3-4-5-7-4-5 |
| 30 | ,, ,, | Yü Chieh Hsing | 7-3-3-7-6-4-4-5; 7-3-3-7-6-4-4-5 |
| 31 | Yeh Ch'ing Ch'en | Ho Sheng Chao | 7-5-7-5; 4-4-5-7-5 |
| 32 | Yen Shu | Wan Ch'i Sha | (See Poem No. 20) |
| 33 | ,, | P'o Chen Tzu | (See Poem No. 27) |
| 34 | Yen Chi Tao | Lin Chiang Hsien | 6-6-7-5-5; 6-6-7-5-5 |
| 35 | Ou Yang Hsiu | Sheng Ch'a Tzu | 5-5-5-5; 5-5-5-5 |
| 36 | ,, | Wan Ch'i Sha | (See Poem No. 20) |
| 37 | ,, | Su Chung Ch'ing | 7-5-6-6; 3-3-3-4-4 |
| 38 | ,, | Nan Ko Tzu | 5-5-7-9; 5-5-7-9 |
| 39 | ,, | Lin Chiang Hsien | (See Poem No. 16) |
| 40 | ,, | Tieh Lien Hua | 7-4-5-7-7; 7-4-5-7-7 |
| 41 | Liu Yung | Yü Lin Ling | 4-4-6-4-4-6-5-3-4-7; 7-3-5-6-3-4-4-8-7-5 |
| 42 | Su Shih | Pu Suan Tzu | 5-5-7-5; 5-5-7-5 |
| 43 | ,, | ,, ,, | See Poem No. 42) |
| 44 | ,, | Tung Hsien Ko | 4-5-7-3-6-3-6; 5-4-7-5-4-3-4-8-9 |
| 45 | ,, | Shui Tiao Ko T'ou | 5-5-6-6-5-5; 3-3-3-4-7-6-6-5-5-5 |
| 46 | ,, | Nien Nu Chiao | 4-3-6-4-3-6-4-4-5-4-6; 6-5-4-4-3-6-4-5-4-6 |
| 47 | ,, | Shui Lung Yin | 6-7-4-4-4-4-4-5-4-6; 6-3-4-4-4-4-4-3-4-6 |
| 48 | Huang T'ing Chien | Ch'ing P'ing Le | (See Poem No. 22) |
| 49 | ,, | Hua T'ang Ch'un | 7-6-7-4; 6-6-7-4 |
| 50 | Ch'in Kuan | I Wang Sun | 7-7-7-3-7 |
| 51 | ,, | Man T'ing Fang | 4-4-6-4-5-6-3-4-3-4-5; 2-3-4-4-5-4-6-3-4-3-4-5 |

| Poem Number | Poet | P'u (tune-title) | Pattern (characters in each line) |
|---|---|---|---|
| 52 | Chou Pang Yen | Shao Nien Yu | 4-4-5-4-5; 3-4-5-4-5 |
| 53 | ,, ,, ,, | Liu Ch'ou | 5-7-4-5-4-5-7-4-4-6-5-4; 4-5-5-3-6-5-4-3-4-3-6-4-3-4-8-4 |
| 54 | Li Ch'ing Chao | Tsui Hua Yin | 7-5-5-4-5; 7-5-5-4-5 |
| 55 | ,, ,, ,, | Sheng Sheng Man | 4-4-6-4-6-3-4-3-3-6; 6-3-6-4-6-6-3-4-3-7 |
| 56 | Yüeh Fei | Man Chiang Hung | 4-3-3-4-4-7-7-3-5-3; 3-3-3-3-5-4-7-7-3-5-3 |
| 57 | Lu Yu | Ch'ai T'ou Feng | 3-3-7-3-3-4-4-1-1-1; 3-3-7-3-3-4-4-1-1-1 |
| 58 | Hsin Ch'i Chi | Ch'ou Nu Erh | 7-4-4-7; 7-4--7 |
| 59 | ,, ,, ,, | Chu Ying T'ai Chin | 3-3-5-4-5-6-4-3-4; 3-6-5-4-5-6-4-3-4 |
| 60 | ,, ,, ,, | Yung Yü Le | 4-4-4-4-5-4-4-3-4-6; 4-5-6-4-4-5-4-4-6-3-4-4 |
| 61 | ,, ,, ,, | Mo Yü Erh | 7-6-7-6-3-3-7-4-5-4-5; 3-6-6-7-6-3-3-7-4-5-4-5 |
| 62 | Chiang K'uei | An Hsiang | 4-5-4-4-7-6-7-7-5; 2-3-5-4-4-7-6-7-6-4 |
| 63 | ,, ,, | Yang Chou Man | 4-4-6-5-5-7-4-3-4-4; 4-3-4-5-4-4-6-3-4-5-6 |
| 64 | ,, ,, | Su Ying | 4-5-4-4-6-7-7-6; 6-5-4-4-4-6-7-7-6 |
| 65 | Liu K'o Chuang | Pu Suan Tzu | (See Poem No. 42) |
| 66 | Wu Wen Ying | Feng Ju Sung | 7-5-7-3-4-6; 7-5-7-3-4-6-6 |
| 67 | Chiang Chieh | I Chien Mei | 7-4-4-7-4-4; 7-4-4-7-4-4 |
| 68 | Sa Tu La | Nien Nu Chiao | 4-3-6-4-3-6-4-4-5-4-6; 6-4-5-4-3-6-4-4-5-4-6 |
| 69 | ,, ,, ,, | Man Chiang Hung | 4-3-4-3-4-4-7-7-3-5-3; 3-3-3-3-5-4-7-7-3-5-3 |
| 70 | Liu Chi (Po Wen) | Yen Erh Mei | 7-5-4-4-4; 7-5-4-4-4 |
| 71 | Na-lan Hsing-te | Ch'ang Hsiang Ssu | 3-3-7-5; 3-3-7-5 |
| 72 | ,, ,, | Hua T'ang Ch'un | (See Poem No. 49) |
| 73 | Tso Fu | Nan P'u | 4-8-6-5-6-8-5-4-5; 6-7-6-5-6-8-5-7 |

*Notes:* 1. A semi-colon denotes the end of a stanza.

2. Underlining of two numbers denotes that they have been represented in different anthologies as forming either one or two lines (i.e. 5-4 indicates that these nine characters form one line in some versions and two lines—of five and four characters respectively—in others).

# APPENDIX IV

## Pronunciation of Chinese Names Occurring in the Poems

Unless otherwise stated, in English 'a' is pronounced as in 'father', 'i' as in 'chin', 'ow' as in 'how', 'u' as in the French 'u'

| Poem | Chinese name | Pronounced in English |
|---|---|---|
| 2. | Ch'in | Chin |
|  | Pa Ling | Ba Ling |
|  | Le-yu-yüan | Ler-yo-üan |
|  | Hsien Yang | Shi-en Yang |
|  | Han | Han |
| 5. | Pien | Bi-en |
|  | Ssu | Ser |
|  | Kua Chou | Gwa Joe |
|  | Wu | Woo |
| 6. | Hsieh | Shi-eh |
| 8. | Sheng | Shung ('u' as in 'bun') |
| 24 | Ch'in Huai | Chin Hwai ('ai' as in 'eye') |
| 27. | Shen | Shun ('u' as in 'bun') |
|  | P'an | Pan |
| 33. | Ch'ing Ming | Ching Ming |
| 36. | Lu Yao | Loo Yow |
| 42. | Chiang-nan | Ji-ang Nan |
| 46. | Chou | Joe |
|  | Chou Yü | Joe U |
|  | Ch'iao | Chi-ow |
| 49. | Hsiao | Shi-ow |
|  | Hsiang | Shi-ang |
| 52. | Ping | Bing |
|  | Wu | Woo |
| 53. | Ch'u | Choo |
| 54. | Ch'ung Yang | Choong Yang |
| 55. | Wu T'ung | Woo Toong |

| Poem | Chinese Name | Pronounced in English |
|---|---|---|
| 56. | Ching K'ang | Jing Kang |
|  | Ho Lan Shan | Her Lan Shan |
| 60. | Sun Chung Mou | Soon Joong Moe ('oe' as in 'Joe') |
|  | Chi Nu | Jee Noo |
|  | Yüan Chia | Yuan Ji-a |
|  | Lang Chü Hsü | Lang Ju Shu |
|  | Yangchow | Yang Joe |
|  | Fo Li | For Lee |
|  | Lien Po | Li-en Bor |
| 61. | Hsiang Ju | Shi-ang Roo |
|  | Kuei Fei | Gway Fay ('a' as in 'day') |
|  | Fei Yen | Fay Yen ('a' as in 'day') |
| 62. | Ho Hsün | Her Shun |
| 63. | Huai | Hwai ('ai' as in 'eye') |
|  | Tu Mu | Doo Moo |
| 64. | Chao Chün | Jow Jun |
| 66. | Ch'ing Ming | Ching Ming |
| 67. | Ch'iu Niang | Chi-oo Ni-ang |
|  | T'ai Niang | Tie Ni-ang |
| 68. | Wu | Woo |
|  | Ch'u | Choo |
|  | Ch'in Huai | Chin Hwai ('ai' as in 'eye') |
| 69. | Wang | Wang |
|  | Hsieh | Shi-eh |
|  | Chiang | Ji-ang |
| 70. | Ch'in Huai | Chin Hwai ('as' as in 'eye') |
|  | Wu Ling | Woo Ling |
| 71. | Yü Kuan | U Gwan |
| 73. | Hsün Yang | Shun Yang |
|  | Chang Chien | Jang Ji-en |

# INDEX

Ah Chiao, 243
Alliteration, 221, 239
Allusions, classical, etc., xii, 218, 219
An Lu Shan, 228
Autumn Moon, Ode to the, 119
Autumn Festival, 7
Azure Tower, 173, 242

Bactrians, 71
Barbarians (see Tartars, Hsiung Nu),
Birds, migration of, 218
Blackcoat Lane, 195, 244
Blue Bridge, 209, 244
Bynner, Witter, 221
Byzantine, Empire, 229

Calligraphy, xii, xiii, 221
Chang Chih Fu, 238
Ch'ang-an, 3, 17, 227, 228, 232
Ch'ang O, 244
Chao, Kingdom of, 240, 241
Chao Chün (see Wang Chao Chün)
Chao Fei Yen, 167, 242
Chao K'uang Yin, 23, 229, 233
Ch'en, Dynasty, 228, 244
Ch'en, Empress, 242, 243
Chi Kung P'o (see Cock Fort)
Chi Lu Sai, 233
Chi Nu, Emperor, 165, 241
Chiang Chieh, 185, 222, 226
Chiang K'uei, 169, 191, 219, 242
Chiang-nan, 113, 237
Ch'iang, tribes, 236
Ch'iao, Little, 121, 238
Ch'ih Pi (Red Cliff), 111, 121, 220, 238
Chin, Dynasty, 191, 227, 230, 232
Chin-ling, 191, 228, 233, 234, 243

Chin-shih, doctorate, 11, 71, 79, 83, 191
Ch'in, Dynasty, state, 7, 227, 240, 242
Ch'in Huai, 61, 193, 195, 235
Ch'in Kuan, 125, 131, 219, 229, 239
Ch'in Kuei, 151, 241
Ch'in Shih Huang Ti, 227
Ch'in Tsung, Emperor, 240
Ching K'ang, Emperor, 153, 240
Ch'ing, Dynasty, 203, 205, 215, 230
Ch'ing Ming, Festival, 87, 183, 236, 243
Ch'iu Niang (see Hsieh Ch'iu Niang)
Chou Pang Yen, 137, 216, 224, 229, 239
Chou Yü, 121, 238
Chu Shu Chen, 236
Chu Yüan Chang, 230
Ch'u, Kingdom, 141, 193, 233, 237, 240, 243
Ch'ü Chi, 181
Ch'ung Yang, Festival, 145, 240
Civil Service, examination system, 214, 215
Classics, Chinese, 214, 227
Clepsydra (see Water Clock)
Cock Fort (Chi Kung P'o), 23, 27, 233
Courtesans, singing girls, 17, 93, 107, 215, 216, 237

Drama, Chinese stage, 230, 238, 243
Duck-weed, 87, 123, 238
Dynasties, Five (see Five Dynasties)

Eunuchs, palace, 230

Fan Ch'eng Ta, 169
Fan Ch'un Jen (Yao Fu), 71

251

Fan Chung Yen, 71, 218, 229, 236
Fei Yen (see Chao Fei Yen)
Five Dynasties, period, 21, 23, 229
Flowers, wearing in the hair, 236, 240

Geese, wild, 41, 57, 73, 147, 201, 219, 235, 236
Genghiz Khan, 191, 230
Giles, H. A., 221
Girdle, 45, 135, 239
Grand Canal, 232
Great Wall, 227
Guitar, 91, 213
Guitar, Song of the, (see P'i P'a Hsing),

Hair, style, 99, (see also Plum Blossom)
Han, Dynasty, 7, 219, 227, 236
Han Lin, Academy, 3, 11, 79
Hangchow, 11, 111, 151, 155, 191, 229, 230, 237
Heng Yang, hills, 236
Ho Hsün, 171, 242
Ho Lan Shan, 153, 241
Hsiang-ju (see Ssu-ma Hsiang-ju)
Hsiang River (see Hsiao River)
Hsiao (and Hsiang) Rivers, 129, 239
Hsiao Hung, 169
Hsiao P'in, 89, 236
Hsiao Tsung, Emperor, 151
Hsieh Ch'iu Niang, 187, 243
Hsien P'ei, 228
Hsien-yang, 7, 227
Hsin Ch'i Chi, 155, 159, 191, 217, 220, 238, 241
Hsiung Nu, 'Barbarians' (see also Tartars), 219, 228, 236, 241, 242
Hsüan Tsung, Emperor, 228, 242
Hsün-yang, 211
Hua Chien Chi, 17
Huai River, 151, 173, 229, 242
Huang T'ing Chien, 125, 225, 229, 232, 239
Huns (see also Tartars), 153
Huo Ch'ü Ping, 241

I Wang Sun, P'u and Music, 133, 219, 247

Jao-Chow, 71

K'ai-feng (see Pien-liang)
Kao Tsung, Emperor, 151, 229
Khitan, Tartar tribe, 229, 230
Kua-chou, 15, 232
Kublai Khan, 230
Kuei Fei (see Yang Kuei Fei)

Lang Chü Hsü, 165, 241
Lang T'ao Sha Man, P'u, 224
Lantern Festival, 95, 236
Lê-yu-yüan, 7, 232
Lei T'ai Shih, 159
Li Ching (and see Li Ying), 23
Li Ch'ing Chao, 143, 229
Li Po, 3, 11, 215, 227, 232
Li Shih Min, 228
Li Shih Shih, 216
Li Te Yü, 243
Li Ying, 23, 29, 83, 229, 232, 233
Li Yü, xii, 23, 29, 218, 219, 224, 226, 229, 233–235
Lien Po, General, 165, 241
Lin Hsiang Ju, 240, 241
Liu Chi (Po Wen), 199, 230
Liu K'o Chuang, 177, 217
Liu Pang, 227
Liu Sung, Dynasty, 241
Liu Yung, 107, 111, 131, 229, 237
Lo Kuan Chung, 238
Lo-yang, 228
Lu Yao, tune, 97, 237
Lu Yu, 155, 159, 241
Lyrics, Chinese (see Tz'u),
Lyrics, English, 214

Macartney, Lord, xi
Manchu, Dynasty (see Ch'ing Dynasty)
Manchu, 205, 230
Manchuria, 205
Mandarin Duck, 101, 183, 237, 243
Meng Ch'ang, 237

Migration, southward of Chinese, 228, 230
Ming, Dynasty, 197, 199, 230, 231
Ming Huang, Emperor (see Hsüan Tsung)
Mongol, Dynasty (see Yüan Dynasty)
Mongol, invasions, 228, 230
Music, 169, 214, 219, 220

Na-lan Hsing-te, 205, 219, 230
Nan T'ang Chung Chu (see Li Ying), 23
Nan T'ang Hou Chu (see Li Yü), 29
Night-jar, 45, 133
Nüchen Tartars, 151, 155, 159, 191, 229, 230, 240
Nü Ying, 239

O Huang, 239
Onomatopoeia, 221, 222, 226
Orioles (golden), 25, 41, 87, 127, 163, 183, 232, 239
Ornamentation, of Chinese Poetry 214–226
Ou Yang Hsiu, 93, 225, 229, 236

Pairing (see Parallelism)
Pan Ch'ao, 236
P'an An Jen, 67, 235
Paper, invention of, 227, 231
Parallelism, pairing, 214, 221, 224, 237
Pattern, tonal, 221, 224
— tune- (see P'u), 223, 245
Peking (see also Yen), 205, 230
Phoenix Tree (see W'u T'ung trees), 51, 115, 234
P'i P'a (Hsing), 211, 244
Pien River, 15, 232
Pien-liang (K'ai Feng), 29, 155, 229, 232
Pillow, 237
P'ing-tse, analysis of tonal pattern, 224
Plum Blossom, in the hair, 99, 175, 218, 237, 243

Plum Blossom, Ode to the, 175
Po Chü I, 11, 211, 232, 244
Porcelain, invention of, 227, 231
Printing, invention of, 228, 231
Pronunciation, of Chinese, 249
P'u, tune-pattern, xiii, 223, 224, 245

Rainbow Skirt, tune, 43, 234
Red Cliff (see Ch'ih Pi),
Rhyme, 214, 221, 222, 239
Rhythm, 221, 223
Rose, Ode to a Red, 141, 240

Sa Tu La, 191, 230, 243
Sachet, perfume, 135, 239
San Kuo Chih Yen I, 238
San Kuo (see Three Kingdoms)
Shen I, 244
Shen Yüeh, 67, 235
Sheng, 27, 139, 216, 233, 234, 240, 243
Shih, 214, 215
Shih Ching, 214
Shou Yang Kung Chu (Princess), 243
Shu, Kingdom of, 237
Shun, Emperor, 239
Six Dynasties, 191, 193, 195, 228, 243
Soochow, 11
Southern Sung, Dynasty, 151, 229
Southern T'ang, Dynasty, 23, 29, 229
Ssu, River, 15, 232
Ssu-ma Hsiang-ju, 167, 242
Staunton, George Thomas, xi
Su Shih (Tung P'o), 111, 125, 131, 220, 225, 229, 237–8
Su Wu, 219
Sui, Dynasty, 228, 244
Sun Chung Mou, 165, 238, 241
Sun Ch'üan (see Sun Chung Mou)
Sun Ts'e, 238
Sung, Dynasty, 23, 69, 215, 218, 224, 227, 229
Sung Dynasty, poets, 226
Sung T'ai Tsu, 23, 29
Sung T'ai Tsung, 29, 235
Swallows, 85, 87, 103, 129, 218

T'ai Niang, 187, 243
T'ai Shih Ling, 199
T'ai Tsung (see Sung T'ai Tsung)
T'ang, Dynasty, 3, 23, 214, 215, 227, 228
Taoist, 3
T'ao Ch'ien, 240
Tartars (see also Barbarians and Hsiung Nu), 71, 155, 173, 175, 228, 230, 241, 242
Three Kingdoms, 121, 228, 238, 241
Tibet, 230, 236
Tones of Chinese Characters, 223, 224
Tou Hsien, 236
Ts'ao Ts'ao, 238
Tso Fu, 211, 230, 244
Tu Mu, 173, 242
Tune Pattern (see P'u)
T'ung Fei, 219
Tungusic, peoples, 228
Turkestan, 227
Turks, 228
Tz'u, vii, xii, 3, 11, 17, 29, 83, 107, 111, 125, 137, 155, 159, 169, 177, 181, 185, 199, 211, 214–26, 227, 229

Wade, system of transliteration, xiii, 220
Waley, Arthur, 220
Wang and Hsieh families, 195, 244
Wang An Shih, 111
Wang Chao Chün, 175, 242, 243
Water-clock (Clepsydra), 19, 115, 232

Wei, Kingdom, of, 238
Wei (T'o-pa), 228
Wei Tsung, Emperor, 240
Well of Shame, 195, 244
Wen T'ing Yün, 17, 181, 223, 232
West(ern) Lake (Hangchow), 151, 171
Whitaker, Dr. K. P. K., 224
Willow Flower, Ode to, 123, 238
Wu, Kingdom of, 15, 139, 193, 216, 238, 241, 243
Wu Tai (see Five Dynasties)
Wu Ti, Emperor (Han), 219, 240, 243
Wu T'ung, trees, 51, 218, 234, 235
Wu Wen Ying, 181, 243

Yang Chien, 228
Yangchow, 165, 191, 229, 242
Yang Kuei Fei, 3, 167, 242
Yeh Ch'ing Ch'en, 79, 229
Yen (Peking), 229
Yen Chi Tao, 89, 229, 236
Yen Jan, hills, 236
Yen Shu, 83, 89, 217, 218, 229, 236
Yü Huan (see Yang Kuei Fei),
Yü Kuan, pass, 207, 244
Yüan, Dynasty, 185, 189, 199, 219, 230
Yüan Chia, Emperor, 165, 241
Yüeh Fei, 151, 155, 159, 191, 226, 229, 240
Yüeh Yün, 151
Yün Ying, 244

For Product Safety Concerns and Information please contact our EU
representative GPSR@taylorandfrancis.com
Taylor & Francis Verlag GmbH, Kaufingerstraße 24, 80331 München, Germany

www.ingramcontent.com/pod-product-compliance
Lightning Source LLC
Chambersburg PA
CBHW070557300426
44113CB00010B/1289